# PUBLIC HOUSING IN ACTION

# THE RECORD OF PITTSBURGH

# PUBLIC HOUSING IN ACTION

## THE RECORD OF PITTSBURGH

ROBERT K. BROWN

Library of Congress Catalog Card Number: 59-11251



Printed in the United States of America

Lithoprinted in U.S.A.
EDWARDS BROTHERS, INC.
Ann Arbor, Michigan

TO

HARRY EARL POPLE, SR.

## FOREWORD

The author wishes to express his appreciation to the many people who aided in the preparation of this study. Mr. Wilson Borland, Mr. Ralph Harkins, Mr. Warren Matson and Mr. Lester Zindel, all staff members of the Housing Authority of the City of Pittsburgh, aided with specific sections of the housing program of the City of Pittsburgh.

This study was written under the guidance of Dr. A. M. Woodruff, Director, Bureau of Business Research, University of Pittsburgh; the author wishes to express unbounded appreciation for his aid and inspiration. Dr. J. A. Crabtree, Dr. A. Isaacs, Dr. H. Rowland and Dr. L. A. Shattuck, members of the Graduate Faculty of the University of Pittsburgh made valuable contributions to the study. Dr. Miles L. Colean, Housing Economist, Washington, D.C., Mr. Patrick J. Cusick, Executive Director, Pittsburgh Regional Planning Commission, and Mr. Bernard E. Loshbough, Executive Director, ACTION-Housing, Inc., offered many valuable and constructive ideas. Grateful appreciation is also extended to my wife, Joanne, and to Mr. and Mrs. Harry E. Pople for their contributions to the completion of this study. Of course, none of those who read the manuscript is responsible for any errors that may appear.

Miss June Humphreys aided in the mechanical preparation of the study. Miss Shirley Lipson edited the manuscript.

Robert K. Brown
Director
Real Estate Program
Georgia State College

Atlanta, 1959

## PREFACE

The problem of substandard housing is not a recent one. Recorded history contains reference to substandard housing in every civilization. The criteria which established the boundary between standard and substandard housing, however, have varied from civilization to civilization, even from center to center in the same era. Many of the dwelling units of the modern-day "slum" would not have been considered substandard in sixteenth century London, nor would they presently be substandard in a poverty-ridden Asian village.

The term "slum" is difficult to define. Characteristically, definitions of a slum have depended on the existence of physical factors as determinants of housing quality.[1] Such definitions have not emphasized the importance of less tangible factors, such as the cleanliness of the individual dwelling unit, the care of the children, the health habits of the residents. As important as these factors are, they have not lent themselves to investigation and classification as readily as the physical factors of housing construction and sanitation facilities. This difficulty still exists today.[2] The common denominator of a slum appears to be the prevalence of dwelling units, within a defined area, which have deteriorated below the community's accepted standard of housing.

The modern slum had its beginning in the rise of industrialism and the concentration of manufacturing facilities and population in central, urban locations. This fostered the tenement structure and overcrowded living conditions; high rents forced families into inadequate facilities which combined to create the modern slum. Housing began to deteriorate below the minimum standard accepted then.

---

1. The United States Housing Act of 1937 defines a slum as ". . . any area where dwellings predominate which, by reason of dilapidation, overcrowding, faulty design, lack of ventilation, light or sanitation facilities, or any combination of these factors, are detrimental to safety, health or morals."
2. See Miles Colean, Renewing Our Cities, Twentieth Century Fund, New York, 1953, pp. 37-39.

The problems of overcrowded housing and unsanitary living conditions, compounded by many years of continued growth, still require a solution. Urban decentralization—the flight of people and commerce to the peripheral areas of an urban center—threatens to transform the present urban-suburban relationship into one where the urban area may lose its present paramount position and become a subsidiary area, lying between various suburban business and residential areas.

Decentralization is also of ancient origin, but its special significance today stems from the relative loss of population by the nation's urban areas. In many ways decentralization holds a promise of a better functional relationship between population and employment if a proper relationship is created and maintained between the city center and the outlying subcenters. The present trend, however, indicates that this balance will not be established until the urban center corrects some of its primary faults, chiefly slums.

## The Object of the Investigation

The object of this study is to investigate the legislative evolution of the public housing program and to illustrate its financial impact, especially on a specific community. Analysis and evaluation proceeds on the assumption that the existing social-economic system provides both criteria of success and analytical tools which are applicable to the problem. These tools have been employed in obtaining such conclusions as seem justifiable.

The time period covered in this study is from 1933, when the Federal Government first committed itself to active participation in a low-rent housing program, through 1956.

## Approach

Part I, the Introduction, contains a brief survey of the legislative evolution of the public housing program. This development is presented with special attention directed toward those factors which influenced the initiation and continuation of the program. The intended purposes of the program and their continuity of application are examined.

Part II deals with an investigation of the financial impact of the public housing program on the city of Pittsburgh, Pennsylvania. The costs of the program are of concern throughout the study, but special attention is focused on the financial problems of the program in terms of this specific community.

With these considerations at hand, Part III presents the evidences of success or shortcoming. This examination will permit the drawing of certain conclusions concerning the success of the public housing program and the presentation of recommendations based on these conclusions.

## CONTENTS

Page

## LIST OF TABLES

## LIST OF FIGURES

Part One

# INTRODUCTION

CHAPTER ONE

# The Legislative Evolution of Public Housing

## The National Industrial Recovery Act

Public housing as it is known today is of relatively recent origin. Except for the building of houses for war workers in 1918, only with the passage of the National Industrial Recovery Act in June of 1933 was provision made for the entry of the Federal Government into the low-rent housing field. Title II of this act provided for the creation of a Federal Emergency Administration of Public Works and directed its administrator to prepare a comprehensive program of public works which was to include, among other things, the "construction, reconstruction, alteration, or repair under public regulation or control of low-cost housing and slum clearance projects." Accordingly, a Housing Division, created within the Public Works Administration, had the responsibility of inaugurating as rapidly as possible this aspect of the overall recovery program. The Housing Division was authorized specifically to institute work relief activities designed to produce, in addition to employment opportunities, low-rent housing projects to accommodate low-income families.

Despite the apparent altruism contained in the creation of this Federally-supported low-rent housing program, clearly the Federal Government would not have entered the low-rent housing field when it did were it not for the desire to stimulate employment in the housing industry through a program of public works. The problem of inadequate sanitary housing for low-income families was far from new, although the depression had aggravated it. The reasons prompting the creation of the Housing Division were not so important, however, to low-rent housing enthusiasts as the simple fact that the program did exist. After many years of fruitless endeavor to obtain Federal Government support of such a program, the depression had prompted the birth of a means whereby theory could be put into application. Once the opportunity to achieve lasting reform had been presented, public housing proponents would not relinquish it by merely participating in the relatively unplanned spending of Federal monies; as the low-rent housing program developed into a recognizable form in the years 1933-1936,[3] a longer-range goal of permanent Government participation was in fact being substituted for spending as the primary purpose of Housing Division officials. Furthered by prevailing economic conditions which seemed to dictate the continuance of Government support, the problem of housing for the low-income group began to receive considerable attention on a national scale.

## The United States Housing Act of 1937

The increasing attention culminated in the enactment of the United States Housing Act of 1937, Public Law 412, and the resultant creation of a semi-permanent Federal public housing agency, the United States Housing Authority. This act transformed an emergency function into a program of quasi-permanent policy. The emergency-relief aspects of its depression predecessor, however, still attached themselves to the program, for it was intended primarily as a continuation of the administration's employment stimulation policies. A corollary function, once again, was the extension of public aid through the clearing of slums and the construction of decent, sanitary dwellings for the nation's economically handicapped families. But a change in the relative importance attached to the economic and humanitarian aspects of the program was noticeable. The humanitarian purpose had increased in importance in 1937 to a plane of equal emphasis with the program's anticipated economic benefits.

By the summer of 1939, the United States Housing Authority had committed all of its authorized funds to various local housing authorities participating in the low-rent housing program. Both its original authorization of $500,000,000.00 and the subsequent authorization in 1938 of $300,000,000.00 had been either earmarked or actually expended.[4] Accordingly, representatives of the United States Housing Authority appeared before the committees of the legislative branches to request an additional appropriation of funds.

3. One important event which helped shape the operating framework of the post-1937 program was the 1935 decision of the U.S. Court of Appeals that, in effect, prevented the Federal Government from condemning land for housing purposes and the subsequent invention of the local authority formula which was to become the backbone of the public housing program. See U.S. v. Certain Lands in City of Louisville, 78 F. (2d) 684, 1935.

4. The USHA was to be given a "trial run" for a period of three years, at the end of which its performance record was to be subject to Congressional review. The legislators provided expressly that no expenditures were to be made beyond the limits of the initial authorizations without the express consent of Congress.

2 continued

The Senate reacted favorably to the functioning of the program, for it approved the requested authorization. But the House Committee on Banking and Currency did not report the bill favorably to the House of Representatives. Its reluctance to approve the amendments proposed was based on two main considerations: the question of the total amount of the obligation the Federal Government would be assuming, and the serious doubt as to whether the Seventy-sixth Congress had the right to bind future Congresses to the payment of these obligations, since the payment of annual subsidies[5] was constructed as a continuing obligation of the Federal Government. This point was of fundamental importance, since it was a further indication of the reluctance of the House of Representatives to guarantee, in effect, the continued flow of Federal funds into the low-rent housing program. It, therefore, reflected House opposition to the concept of permanent Government participation in such a program.

In addition, the prospects for complete economic recovery had increased considerably since the previous year when Congress had granted the United States Housing Authority an additional $300,000,000.00 authorization. The prevailing philosophy seemed to be that the program had fulfilled its purpose. The permanent aspects of the program, beyond the completion of projects already authorized, seemed to have diminished as economic activity and prospects for prosperity had increased.

The hopes and efforts of those most interested in the perpetuation of Government financial aid to a low-rent public housing program appeared to be frustrated. But catastrophe and misfortune appeared once again to take the program in hand and reactivate it as an important Government activity. The emphasis of the program was changed, however, to accommodate the housing emergency which came with World War II.

## Public Law 671

By the end of the nineteen-thirties, the leaders of the United States were aware of the very real possibility that their country would be drawn into a second world war and that a critical shortage of housing existed in many prime defense production areas. A means was needed to provide the necessary housing in the shortest possible time; the most logical course was to utilize existing channels to their fullest capacity. Accordingly, Congress passed legislation in the Summer of 1940, permitting the United States Housing Authority to use its remaining authorization of funds to construct projects for defense

5. The primary method of administering aid to low-income families was to be in the form of annual contributions made by the Federal Government to help maintain low rentals in the projects. Local communities were required to contribute also; their share of the subsidy contribution usually took the form of tax-exemption for low-rent projects.

workers.[6] Further, Congress authorized priorities in the deliveries of materials necessary for such construction as was undertaken by the United States Housing Authority for the provision of dwellings for defense workers.

For the low-rent housing program, this Congressional order was a last minute reprieve, for Congress's failure to grant an additional fund authorization during 1939 seemed a definite indication of reluctance to consider the program as a permanent Government activity. The public housing program would probably have ceased to exist insofar as future authorizations were concerned, had it not been for the advent of the war and the creation, or re-creation, of a defense need for the services of the United States Housing Authority and its low-rent housing program. True, the low-rent housing program was required to surrender the basic principle of low-rentals and low-income tenants, but that must have seemed a small price to pay in view of the guarantee of perpetuation and growth during the war period. In the interim between the outbreak of war and the coming of victory and peace, the addition of units and the authorization of funds could do no worse than strengthen the relative bargaining position of the low-rent housing program for the postwar period.

## The Post-World War II Period

The seven year period of 1937-1944 had wrought a social revolution in terms of what had transpired, or had not transpired, before it. The low-rent housing program had taken giant steps during this period.[7] Rather than having lost significance during World War II, the program had increased considerably in physical stature, if not social importance.

Certainly, if any group looked to the postwar period with confidence, the public housing advocates[8] must have felt at least a high degree of

6. Public Law 671, 76th Congress, June 28, 1940. Under the terms of this legislation, the housing constructed was to be a permanent type, for most of the units subsequently occupied were already in advanced planning stages or under actual construction by local authorities. Provision was made in the law whereby the housing units constructed under Public Law 671 would revert to the local housing authorities at the termination of the war emergency. Management of the "671 projects" was entrusted to the local housing authorities, which were charged with the responsibility of letting space at fair market rentals prevailing in the local community for private housing of like kind and quality. Preference for tenancy was to be given to defense workers.
7. By December 31, 1945, a total of 172,503 active dwelling units had been programmed under the United States Housing Act; these included 119,965 Public Law 412 low-rent units and 52,538 units programmed under the Defense Amendment, Public Law 671. National Housing Agency, Fourth Annual Report, 1945 (Washington: U.S. Government Printing Office, 1945), pp. 126, 129.
8. See: Robert K. Brown, Public Housing Legislation—An Interpretation, Bureau of Business and Economic Research, Georgia State College, Atlanta, 1959, for a detailed analysis of the individuals and interests identified here as "public housing advocates."

quiet optimism. Not only had the program grown in size and importance when measured in terms of the existing physical investment, but also a definite and ascertained demand existed in many urban areas for an immediate expansion of the program. Beginning in late 1945, however, and continuing through the years 1946, 1947, and 1948, Congressional public housing proponents and private pressure groups sought in vain to secure Congressional approval of additional fund authorizations for the low-rent housing program. The 1945, 1946, and 1947 housing bills incorporated the public housing provisions as one part of an over-all recommended housing program which encompassed the whole of Government housing activities, including the proposed creation of a central, peacetime Government housing agency.[9]

Despite the strong bi-partisan sponsorship of Senators Ellender, Wagner, and Taft, and repeated Senate approval, these postwar housing bills failed to be enacted primarily because of Congressional reluctance to authorize expansion of the low-rent housing program. In 1949, however, a combination of circumstances led, finally, to such expansion,[10] for the Housing Act of 1949, Public Law 171, authorized the addition of 810,000 units of new public housing space over a six-year period.

Public Law 171 was, essentially, an extension by amendment of the low-rent housing program initiated in 1937. Few changes were made in the operating framework of the program. Therefore, the 1949 authorizations might have seemed at the time as a stamp of Congressional approval, a mandate for Government participation on a permanent basis. The circumstances which influenced program expansion, however, seemed to belie such an assumption. The Government attitude toward program growth became even more evident during 1950 and in the ensuing years, 1951-1957.

Operations of the Public Housing Administration were disrupted during 1950 by the outbreak of the Korean War and the subsequent

---

9. The National Housing Agency had been created by Executive Order of the President 9070, February 24, 1942, as coordinating agency for all wartime Government housing activities. One of its constituent agencies, the Federal Public Housing Authority, replaced and assumed the functions of the USHA. Subsequently, the FPHA was replaced in 1947 by the present agency, the Public Housing Administration.

10. Chief among these was the desire of some Congressional members, particularly in the House, to secure additional fund authorizations for the Federal Housing Administration program. This could be achieved only by the enactment of the whole housing program. In addition, a temporary change in House rules allowed the proponents of the bill to call it to the House floor despite Rules Committee opposition. Third, opposition to the creation of a central Government housing agency, which contributed to the defeat of prior postwar housing bills, had been nullified by the creation on July 27, 1947, of the Housing and Home Finance Agency. Fourth, the stature of President Truman had been enhanced considerably by his election victory: this contributed, hypothetically, to the enactment of Public Law 171.

issuance of a Presidential directive on July 18, 1950, which restricted the start of construction of the new units authorized by Public Law 171. Afterwards, the addition of these units was curtailed repeatedly by the refusal of Congress to re-endorse full-scale program expansion.[11] As of December 31, 1957, the Public Housing Administration still had not constructed all of the units authorized in 1949.

The public housing program, therefore, has never been given a popular mandate by Congress at any time during the program's existence. Postwar Congressional debates illustrate graphically the trend toward an ever-increasing reluctance to endorse additional loan and annual contributions fund authorizations for public housing. The controversy continues to grow as the public housing program is being beset by perhaps its greatest potential adversary—rising incomes.[12]

Created during the greatest economic calamity to ever befall this nation, public housing had as its initial purpose the fulfillment of an emergency need. In succeeding years the existence of other emergency situations seemed to dictate program continuation; available evidence indicates that program expansions were not effected primarily because of social motivations, but by the desire to achieve other economic goals. During the post-World War II era, a substantial number of Congressmen strongly resisted the postwar expansion of the program. Although new authorizations were finally obtained, strong anti-public housing sentiment continued to find expression in Congress. The primary criticism seemed to be that the program was not suited to the present economic climate. At least a portion of this sentiment must have emanated from the inalterable fact that the program's purposes and functions could not be re-equated to existing economic and social conditions, because no clear-cut definition of them had ever been made and applied. This condition was due primarily to the circumstances which had prompted the creation and expansion of the program. If it had been intended primarily as a means of social improvement, some consistency of operation could have been achieved.

---

11. Limitations were effected or continued in force by the Independent Office Appropriations Acts of 1951, 1952, and 1953. In addition, the Housing Acts of 1954 and 1955, although permitting the addition of new units, restricted program expansion by authorizing units significantly below the numbers desired by the Public Housing Administration. Whenever Congress did retreat from this position, such as in the Housing Act of 1956, it did continue Government aid to "private-use" housing programs, such as the F.H.A. No marked change occurred in its social sentiment toward the public housing program.
12. Project tenants are governed by income-rent ratios. Rising incomes tend to create vacancies in projects if they are not taken into account. Some authorities, however, foresee the time when this trend toward a general rising income level will negate the necessity for public housing aid. Others believe that, inevitably, some families will require aid. In any event, rigidity in rent-income ratios will present acute problems for the administrators of the public housing program as long as prosperity and inflation continue to push incomes upward.

Instead, because of its sporadic expansions and contractions and its utilization as a special use function of Government, the program has failed to achieve much success in its social objectives.

The problems of over-crowded and unsanitary living conditions, compounded by many years of continued growth, still require solution. During the 25-year existence of the public housing program, local communities have constructed approximately 500,000 units of low-rent housing space. A corollary activity of this construction, by virtue of the requirements governing the program, has been the clearing of slums and blighted areas. Yet, after what would seem to be an adequate period of experimentation, the nation's urban areas still contain acres of slum dwellings.

Fortunately, the public housing program is not a new venture. Operating statistics and related information are readily available for analysis. Society must re-evaluate its efforts, on the basis of success to date, if a realistic and consistent approach in keeping with the capabilities of a community's resources is to be made toward slum eradication. In the final analysis, logic demands the objective analysis of the program in terms of its impact on localities in which projects are located, since the evidence of success or failure, in terms of actual achievement, exist here. The following study presents a portion of this impact on one local community.

Part Two

# FINANCIAL IMPACT OF THE PROGRAM ON PITTSBURGH

CHAPTER TWO

# Housing for the Low-Income Group in Pittsburgh

The public housing program has had financial impact on Pittsburgh from the very inception of the Housing Authority of the City of Pittsburgh.[13] The years since its inception in 1937 have witnessed an intensification of this impact as new projects have been planned and built. Each new unit of public housing space has increased the amount of capital investment in Pittsburgh real property and has provided a new outlet for investment through purchase of the Authority's long term bond issues; each new unit has afforded additional employment opportunities for those connected with project planning, development, and construction.

In succeeding pages the addition of these units will be presented chronologically to establish some rationale for investigation of the need for, and presumably, the reason for the continued addition of public housing units. The primary objective of the public housing program, at least from the local community's point of view, would seem to be the provision of decent, sanitary housing for at least a significant portion of the community's low-income[14] population.

Specifically, the financial impact of one public housing program will be measured in dollar amounts in terms of the direct investment in land and structures and improvements; in terms of the preliminary and permanent financing of the debt incurred by reason of the construction of the public housing projects; in terms of subsidy contributions made by the Federal government; and in terms of subsidy

13. When capitalized in this paper, the term "Authority" will refer to the Housing Authority of the City of Pittsburgh.

14. A low-income family, for the purposes of this study, is defined as one whose income, housing needs, and family size make it eligible for public housing. See Appendix I, pages 156-158 for the Authority's tenant eligibility requirements.

payments made by the local community's residents by reason of the property tax provisions of the United States Housing Act of 1937, as amended.[15]

The accurate measurement of the additions to dilapidated housing[16] caused by the constant operation of functional and physical obsolescence and the resultant "filtering-down" of rental properties within the income reach of low-income families is virtually impossible. This process is accelerated because the protracted absence of adequate repairs in many areas already inhabited by low-income families seems to be a safe assumption. In any event, the relationship between the total population's percentage of low-income families and the percentage increase or decrease in the available supply of low-rental housing units can be measured quantitatively. The hypothesis is that if the percentage of low-income families has risen and the number of available units has remained stable or declined, the public housing program has failed to achieve thus far at least one of its stated objectives; that being ". . . the provision of decent, safe, and sanitary dwellings for families of low income."[17]

Ultimately, only one method can appraise objectively the achievements of the public housing program in the city of Pittsburgh. Regardless of the moral intent and social purpose of any individual or group of individuals, their achievements and the continuation of a given program must be considered within the framework of financial actualities. If the financial expenditures and responsibilities involved in the creation, growth, and maintenance of the program are justified by the results achieved, a reasonable conclusion would seem to be, in the writer's opinion, that the program's existence is justified.

* * * * * * * * * *

By 1940, after a half-century of industrial expansion, Pittsburgh had become a dirty, middle-aged city, proud of its industrial achievements, but at least a little ashamed of its soot-covered buildings and the squalor of its substandard housing areas.

Pittsburgh had lived through prosperous times when her factories had poured out millions of tons of steel ingots for a large percentage of the world's steel users and the name "Pittsburgh" became synonomous with steel prosperity. Unfortunately, steel prosperity meant other things for Pittsburgh. The high degree of industrialism achieved, as one of its by-products, had concentration of a great many people in a relatively small area, for industrial mechanization demanded a large and ready labor supply, and since the public transportation fa-

15. Public Law 412, 75th Congress, 1st Sess., 1937.
16. The United States Bureau of the Census defines a dwelling unit as "dilapidated," ". . . when it is run-down, neglected, or is of inadequate original construction, so that it does not provide adequate shelter or protection against the elements or it endangers the safety of the occupants."
17. Ibid.

cilities were limited, workers' homes had to be close to the factories.

As the number of workers increased, greater and greater strain was placed on the available housing supply and any additions to this supply were quickly absorbed by the great mass of shelter-seekers. The result was a continual down-grading of housing and housing standards in many residential areas within the city limits. The increasing popularity of life in the suburbs gave positive testimony to this decline of the city and the increasing unpopularity of its residential areas. A mighty social revolution was taking place, and Pittsburgh, along with other major American cities, was caught by it. Only positive action would halt the slide, if it were to be halted at all.

Pittsburgh's civic leaders did begin to initiate programs aimed at eradication of her industrial blight in an effort to help their city "turn the corner" and start the long climb back to cleanliness. Many facets of the problem of municipal decay demanded attention, among them smoke control and rejuvenation of the downtown area; but none demanded more immediate attention than that of housing conditions, particularly housing for the city's low-income portion of the population.

Efforts to eradicate the slums and upgrade the quality of residential dwellings in Pittsburgh took many forms. The greatest single program provided low-rent housing through the media of the Federal public housing program.

Pittsburgh's first public housing unit was occupied officially on July 15, 1940.[18] No evaluation of the results of the public housing program would be complete without a description of previous housing conditions. The decade 1930-1940 will be used to illustrate the magnitude of the problem which the public housing program was designed to ameliorate. The first substantial efforts of the municipal government to improve substandard housing occurred during this same period.

## Housing for the Low-Income Group: 1930-1933

The Pittsburgh Housing Association,[19] established in 1929, concentrated in its early years upon housing inspection in the poorer sections

---

18. Housing Authority of the City of Pittsburgh, The First Seven Years, Pittsburgh, p. 19.
19. The Pittsburgh Housing Association is a civic organization founded in 1929 to study, inform, stimulate and encourage the citizens of Pittsburgh in their fight for the alleviation of sub-standard housing and its many bad side effects. The Association has no law-enforcing or law-enacting powers. Its role in the community has been one of "stimulator" and, in some cases, "participant." Its studies of housing conditions, which have been published periodically have supplemented the Association's agitation for housing reform. The analysis of the period 1930-1940, contained in this study, is based on these periodic reports.

of the city. With the first-hand data thus collected, the Association hoped to accelerate the correction of violations of existing sanitary and building codes. These violations were reported to the proper officials and subsequent reinspections were made by the Association until the violations were corrected. The efforts were reasonably successful, for out of a total of 1,328 violations reported by the Association during 1930, 926, or 69.7 per cent, were corrected.[20]

In the period 1929-1933, the percentage of violations reported and corrected increased appreciably,[21] and statistics indicated considerable progress. These statistics, however, did not reveal the total situation. Although the number of violations reported as corrected was valid, the statistics did not reveal the important fact that the most serious violations were not being remedied. Housing situations had been affected by the Great Depression. Investigation revealed that rental payments to landlords were falling sharply; consequently, landlords, who ordinarily would have made repairs, had neither the funds nor the inclination to make them.

Depression times were reflected in another way. The Association's report of 1930 had hinted at government subsidization of housing construction as a possible depression cure.[22] The report issued in 1933 went several steps further. In it, the Association questioned the adequacy of private enterprise in combating the spread of the slum areas. Further, the tremendous financial and social cost of slum areas to a city was becoming increasingly evident, and private enterprise, as owner of these areas, was taking the blame. The question was asked, "Is it (private enterprise) as important as it seems to be? Slum owners today are subsidized by other taxpayers, for what the slum pays in taxes is only a fraction of what it costs in public services. Must this subsidy be continued in order that conditions economically and socially demoralizing may be continued?"[23] The Association's answer, in the negative, was complete with suggestions for an alternative program which embodied, on the local level, the same "make-work" principles which were to be soon employed on a national scale.[24]

The Association's alternative program supported the demolition of the city's worst housing wrecks, for "Ridding the city of the worst of its housing . . . at least alleviated unemployment . . . cleared sites for future building and decreased fire and sanitary hazards."[25] The demolition of unsanitary and unsafe houses was coupled with the

20. Pittsburgh Housing Association, Housing in Pittsburgh, 1931-1933 (Pittsburgh, 1933), p. 4.
21. Ibid., p. 11.
22. Pittsburgh Housing Association, Housing in Pittsburgh, 1930 (Pittsburgh, 1931, p. 8.
23. Pittsburgh Housing Association, Housing in Pittsburgh, 1931-1933 (Pittsburgh, 1933), p. 11.
24. Ibid., p. 17.
25. Ibid.

advocacy of seeking slum clearance assistance on the state or national levels.[26] Special mention was made of the creation of the Housing Division of the Public Works Administration and the possibility of aid from it provided the initiative in slum clearance.[27] Public housing was still spoken of in vague terms. "Even though so much has been promised in the realm of public housing and yet so little accomplished in actual fact, our interest, although still academic, is none the less real."[28]

This attitude in Pittsburgh seems similar to the motives which prompted Congress to enter the field of low-rent housing: the need to boost employment in the construction industry coupled with the desire of some citizens for Federal assistance in the fight against the slum. Locally, as nationally, speed was regarded as essential.[29]

The Association had endeavored to secure passage of legislation by the state in the early 1930's so that cities, such as Pittsburgh, might take advantage of Federal recovery assistance.[30] Beginning in 1931, interested persons joined in a movement spearheaded by the Pittsburgh Housing Association aimed at securing the creation of a state housing board. The proposed legislation also provided for the creation of limited-dividend corporations to be financed primarily by loans from the Reconstruction Finance Corporation.

The proposed bills were introduced in the special session of the legislature in 1932 and both in the regular and in the special sessions of 1933. When the bills were reintroduced in the special session of 1933, a further proviso called for the creation of public housing authorities. Neither this provision nor the previous ones met with legislative approval. According to the Pittsburgh Housing Association, "failure was primarily due to Philadelphia opposition,"[31] particularly private real estate interests which were fearful of the possible consequences of the right of eminent domain.

## Housing for the Low-Income Group: 1934-1937

Poor housing was demolished in the period 1934-1937 at the rate of more than 500 dwelling units per year.[32] Noticeable changes could be seen in some neighborhoods where vacant lots dotted the hillsides.

Economic recovery brought increased employment, and families that had been forced to double-up were beginning to acquire the

---

26. Ibid., p. 18.
27. Ibid., p. 19.
28. Pittsburgh Housing Association, Housing in Pittsburgh, 1934-1937 (Pittsburgh, 1937), p. 5.
29. Ibid.
30. See: Pittsburgh Housing Association, Housing in Pittsburgh, 1931-1933 (Pittsburgh, 1934), p. 22.
31. Ibid.
32. Pittsburgh Housing Association, Housing in Pittsburgh, 1934-1937.

economic means to reestablish their own households. The result was an increased demand for housing. Since few new homes had been built since the twenties, the growing pressure led to rental of quarters that in many cases did not meet even the most minimum health and sanitation requirements. The rental market reacted characteristically as rental values of substandard dwellings rose out of proportion to the accommodations.

The Real Property Inventory of Allegheny County, taken by the University of Pittsburgh in 1937, placed the number of dwelling units which needed to be replaced or completely renovated at 55,000.[33] Demolition over the previous four-year period had decreased the existing housing supply by 2,900 units; only 1,230 units had been added by new construction.[34] As a result, the tenant had to pay a higher rental for over-crowded dwelling space. The average rental of $4.34 per unit paid for slum housing in 1937 reflected an increase of 17 per cent over the corresponding 1936 figure.[35]

The degree of over-crowding was especially acute for Pittsburgh's negro population which faced social barriers in addition to income limitations. By 1937, 45 per cent of the city's negro population was concentrated in the Third and Fifth Wards, in the area called the "Hill District."[36] Since negroes faced special restrictions, negro rental costs rose accordingly. An Association study conducted in 1937 indicated that negroes paid $4.40 per room per month for dwelling space that was in worse condition than that rented by white families for $4.23 per room per month.[37]

Demolition of unfit dwellings increased in the period 1934-1937, as compared to the previous four-year period 1930-1933. The yearly average for 1934-1937 was approximately 500 units demolished, whereas the yearly average for the period 1930-1933 was approximately 98 demolitions.[38]

The Real Property Inventory of Allegheny County also revealed that the city was demolishing a greater number of the most objectionable dwellings than in previous years.[39] One-half the structures demolished were unfit for occupancy, and another one-third of the demolished

33. Real Property Inventory of Allegheny County, University of Pittsburgh, Bureau of Business Research, 1937, p. 89.
34. Pittsburgh Housing Association, Housing in Pittsburgh, 1934-1937 (Pittsburgh, 1937), p. 18.
35. Ibid., p. 10.
36. Ibid., p. 15.
37. Ibid.
38. Pittsburgh Housing Association, Housing in Pittsburgh, 1931-1933 (Pittsburgh, 1933), p. 17 and Housing in Pittsburgh, 1934-1937 (Pittsburgh, 1937), p. 19.
39. The demolitions were undertaken by the Bureau of Building Inspection. Some of the dwellings demolished had been condemned, and some were demolished at the request of the owners.

structures needed major repairs.[40] The demolitions were not restricted to any particular sized house, although 78 per cent of the dwellings demolished were small units designed for one-family use and another 13 per cent had, ". . . undoubtedly been built for one-family use."[41]

The immediate result of the demolitions was to force the occupants of these dwellings to seek other quarters.[42] Some of the occupants probably secured a better grade of accommodations and paid an increased rental in return, although the majority probably moved into other unfit dwelling units. Nevertheless, the net result was some upgrading of available housing, caused by the removal of several thousand of the worst dwelling units from the available rental market.

Another result of the demolitions was to make available a large amount of vacant land possibly adaptable to some municipally profitable use.[43] For the most part, however, new residential building continued to shift to the suburbs. By the end of 1937, only 142 of the 590 sites vacated by demolition had been occupied; of the 142, only two had been used for residential purposes.[44] The widely scattered nature of these sites and their consequent unsuitability for any sizable building venture was one obvious reason for the reluctance of private owners to utilize them. Accordingly, the Association urged the city government to use certain vacant areas for recreation, since safe play space was needed in the highly populated areas—where the greatest number of demolitions had occurred.

Several obstacles were in the way of effective municipal action on the various phases of the housing problem. For one thing, authority over housing matters was divided among so many departments that enforcement of sanitary and satisfactory housing codes was difficult. In addition, irregular employment and considerable economic distress increased the difficulty.

Any concrete program of large size seemed to call for public aid. The Association and certain other civic groups continued to advocate legislation authorizing public loans for low-rent housing construction.[45] Though similar attempts had failed in 1932 and 1933, when measures aimed at enabling Pennsylvania to share in Federal recovery funds were defeated in the state legislature, the Association applied increased pressure in an effort to secure the enactment of such legislation.

---

40. Pittsburgh Housing Association, Housing in Pittsburgh, 1934-1937 (Pittsburgh, 1937), p. 21.
41. Ibid., p. 20.
42. Not all of the dwellings were occupied at the time of demolition. The Association estimated that 41 per cent were vacant in 1934, 53 per cent were occupied by tenants, and the remaining 6 per cent by owners.
43. Pittsburgh Housing Association, Housing in Pittsburgh, 1934-1937 (Pittsburgh, 1937), p. 22.
44. Ibid., p. 24.
45. Ibid., p. 8.

*The United States Housing Act of 1937.*

By 1937 the Federal public housing program had passed the experimental phase which had characterized its beginnings. The program had become integral to the New Deal recovery plan, and at the end of 1937, approximately 20,000 units of low-rental housing had been constructed by direct subsidy of the Federal government.[46] The 1937 plan provided for Federal financial aid, not the complete Federal control of the Public Works Administration. Financial aid was available to legally constituted local public housing authorities; the basic requirement was that the local community have a housing authority under a permissive state law.[47]

*Pennsylvania Housing Legislation: 1937.*

The passage of the Pennsylvania State Enabling Law in 1937 paved the way for the creation of local housing authorities with the power to apply for Federal financial assistance in their community's low-rent housing program.[48] The passage of virtually the same legislation which public housing proponents had been advocating unsuccessfully for five years was due partly to the Legislature's desire to enable Pennsylvania cities to share in the newly-created low-rent housing program. In addition, and of no less significance, the 1937 Legislature was Democrat-controlled; passage of the law represented a marked departure from the many years of Republican domination of the Pennsylvania Government.

In addition, two other housing acts were passed as part of an overall 1937 housing program. The first was the Housing Cooperation Law,[49] ". . . which permits local governments to aid housing authorities by means of loans, donations, and services and which authorizes contracts relating to such aid."[50] The second was the State Board of Housing Law,[51] which created a State Board of Housing to supervise and regulate various state housing agencies, ". . . including local housing authorities."[52]

*The Housing Authority of the City of Pittsburgh.*

The Housing Authority of the City of Pittsburgh was established late in 1937, in compliance with the terms of Pennsylvania's Enabling Act,

46. George Herbert Gray, Housing and Citizenship, A Study of Low-Cost Housing (New York: Reinhold Publishing Corporation, 1946), p. 37.
47. U.S. Department of the Interior, U.S. Housing Authority, What the Housing Act Can Do for your City (Washington: U.S. Government Printing Office, 1938), p. 17.
48. Housing Laws of Pennsylvania, 1937, p. 955.
49. Ibid., p. 888.
50. M. Nelson McGeary, The Pittsburgh Housing Authority, (State College: The Pennsylvania State College, 1943), p. 4.
51. Housing Laws of Pennsylvania, 1937, p. 1705.
52. McGeary, op. cit., p. 4.

under the direction of a five-member board.[53] It qualified to receive Federal financial assistance under the 1937 Federal Act and was to initiate Pittsburgh's public housing program and manage the projects. The creation of the Authority was considered a big advance by those most interested in the housing problems of the low-income group. The 1939 report of the Pittsburgh Housing Association stated that, "... the most spectacular event (of the year prior to 1938) was the passage of State and Federal housing legislation, the establishing of the Housing Authority of the City of Pittsburgh late in 1937 and the gradual shaping of its program in the early months of 1938."[54]

Pittsburgh's demolition program through the depression years had made a distinct contribution to housing progress, for the number of unfit houses demolished was an important, though negative phase of housing progress in Pittsburgh. The 1937 Housing Act accelerated the demolition program by requiring a community to eliminate one unfit dwelling for each new structure built with the aid of Federal funds.

> Within one year from the date of physical completion of the project, the City will eliminate by demolition, condemnation and effective closing or compulsory repair or improvement, unsafe or unsanitary dwellings, at least equal in number to (a) the number of new dwellings to be provided by the Project less (b) the number of unsafe or unsanitary dwellings eliminated from the site of the Project during the development thereof.[55]

This "equivalent elimination" provision was met with mixed emotions by housing economists, some of whom felt it might produce a net housing shortage for the low-income group.

In 1938 the Association emphasized the need for "... more attention being given to use of existing police powers in enforcing both repairs to and demolition of unfit dwellings."[56] The Association felt that effective housing progress had to include provisions to halt the existing blight. Building new dwelling units for the low-income group was not enough unless effective administration and enforcement of housing codes on the local level were also provided.

## Housing for the Low-Income Group: 1938-1940

The Association continued its investigation in 1938, with a total of 897 first inspections and 2,410 follow-up inspections.[57] New properties listed with public departments for the first time numbered 194; new

53. Pittsburgh City Council. Ordinance No. 338, August 26, 1937.
54. Pittsburgh Housing Association, Summary of Major Activities, 1938. (Pittsburgh, 1939), p. 1.
55. Resolution authorizing the issuance of Housing Authority bonds (First Issue) of the Housing Authority of the City of Pittsburgh in the principal amount of Sixteen Million Nine Hundred Forty-Six Thousand Dollars ($16,946,000) for the development of a low-rent housing project and purposes incidental thereto.
56. Pittsburgh Housing Association, Summary of Major Activities, 1938, p. 4.
57. Ibid., p. 9.

violations totaled 1,395.[58] Also in 1938, 2,593 violations previously reported were found corrected; a total of 504 dwelling structures were demolished in various sections of the city, and in the Hill area, 70 of the old structures, which stood on the site of the Authority's first proposed low-rent project, Bedford Dwellings, were razed by the Authority.[59] Two hundred twelve, or 40 per cent of all demolitions were within the confines of three census tracts: the Hill, Hazelwood, and the Lower North Side.[60]

The average rental paid for substandard units equaled $16.00 per unit in 1938, continuing the upward trend begun in 1935.[61] By 1938 occupancy had reached a new high of 98 per cent.[62] The low-income group was paying a higher price than ever before for a constantly diminishing supply of space.

The occupancy of substandard units continued to rise in 1938, to a new record of 98.5 per cent.[63] At this point, however, rents for the average unit did tend to level off.

The high rate of demolition begun in 1934 continued in 1939 when 792 residential structures came down; 483 of the structures demolished were located in the areas of future public housing sites and of other public improvements.[64]

The new public housing program had affected the demolition program in two ways. First of all, previous demolitions had been accomplished without any organized plan other than that of tearing unfit houses down, whereas the 1938 and 1939 demolitions had a definite purpose—to clear large areas for public improvement, especially for the forthcoming public housing projects. This concentration of demolitions also resulted in removing some structures in fairly good condition. Yet elsewhere in the city many unsafe houses were escaping destruction because the public improvement program temporarily accentuated the shortage of housing for the low-income group. Families displaced by demolitions faced a restricted rental market, and many moved into adjacent quarters no better than they had previously occupied. The Association hoped that this situation would be alleviated when the Authority properties were ready for occupancy.[65]

In order to get Federal Assistance under the 1937 Housing Act, Pittsburgh, after creation of the local authority, had to show that many low-income families could not afford available private housing and that additional low-rent housing was needed. Such studies were conducted by the local authority.

58. Ibid., p. 6.
59. Ibid.
60. Ibid.
61. Ibid., p. 7.
62. Ibid.
63. Pittsburgh Housing Association, Housing in Pittsburgh, 1939 (Pittsburgh, 1940), p. 9.
64. Ibid., p. 13.
65. Ibid.

As mentioned above, The 1934 Real Property Inventory had revealed that some 6,400 families lived in substandard houses, that 22,366 dwelling units in Pittsburgh needed major repairs, and that 56,491 structures were rated as substandard. By 1939 the Authority found, on the basis of a sample survey, that 15 per cent of the homes rated as standard in 1934 were substandard.[66] This increase was substantiated by the census of 1940, which found that of Pittsburgh's 179,867 dwelling units, 78,238, or 43.5 per cent, showed characteristics usually defined as substandard.[67]

By 1940 Pittsburgh had the dubious national distinction of having worse housing conditions than any other major American city. Thus, Pittsburgh had at least as much justification for public housing as any other city of comparable size in the United States. In the period 1930-1940 the available housing supply for the low-income group had undergone no marked improvement. The statistics indicated that the deficiency of decent housing quarters had grown worse during this period. The Authority's report concluded with the statement that "It is very obvious that private construction has not kept pace with the housing needs of the growing Pittsburgh population."[68]

*Initial Financing of the Authority.*

The first meeting of the Authority was held on October 11, 1937;[69] its initial request for Federal assistance in the construction of Bedford Dwellings and Addison Terrace was approved by President Roosevelt during June, 1938.[70] In the interim, the Authority's operating expenses were paid for from the proceeds of a $40,000.00 loan from the city of Pittsburgh.[71] Although at first only $7,496,000.00 was approved for the project, in October of 1938 an additional $9,877,000.00 was approved for Wadsworth and Allequippa Terraces.[72]

66. The Housing Authority of the City of Pittsburgh, op. cit., p. 5.
67. U.S. Bureau of the Census, U.S. Census of Population: 1940. Vol. II, Housing-General Characteristics, Part IV. (Washington: U.S. Government Printing Office, 1943), p. 1005.
68. Ibid., pp. 11-12. A more correct statement would be that private enterprise had failed to make a substantial contribution, since a significantly large number of new units would have to be built during any specific year to offset the "filtering down" process which occurs continually on existing housing. Depression conditions precluded the addition of a substantial number of new units during the decade 1930-1940.
69. Ibid., p. 9.
70. Ibid., p. 14.
71. The Housing Authority of the City of Pittsburgh, op. cit., p. 10.
72. McGeary, op. cit., p. 14.

CHAPTER THREE

# Public Housing in Pittsburgh

## The First Venture

Construction was started in December, 1938, on Bedford Dwellings, and the first tenant moved in July 15, 1940. Located on the crest of a ridge high above the Allegheny River, the project was to contain 420 dwelling units on slightly more than 18 acres.[73] The site was acquired at a cost of $313,014.23, and $366,854.21 was expended on site improvements, making a total land investment of $679,868.44.[74]

The Authority's second project, Addison Terrace, was completed in December, 1940 with an additional 802 units.[75] The site for this project cost $456,940.48 plus $1,065,726.91 for site improvements, or a total of $1,522,667.39.[76]

In both cases, the Authority's purchase of hilltop land was an expression of its belief that

> The hills of Pittsburgh, high above the stacks of the steel plants, can become the best part of the city. Housing and planning experts see them as the living place for most of the population, with much of the slopes converted to parks and parkways and the lower levels used as now for commerce and industry. The Pittsburgh Housing Authority takes natural pride in sponsoring a trend toward living where the sun shines the whole day and the pounding of the mills is only a far echo.[77]

This belief was evidenced once again when, the following year, adjoining Addison Terrace, Allequippa Terrace was completed, the most

73. See Appendix II, p.
74. Ibid.
75. Ibid.
76. Ibid.
77. Pittsburgh Housing Authority, op. cit., p. 3.

ambitious undertaking of the Authority, containing 1,851 dwelling units.[78] The site cost of $1,308,645.55 plus $2,277,975.74 spent on direct improvement made a total land investment of $3,586,621.29.[79]

*The Financing of the First Three Projects*

The United States Housing Act of 1937 was designed as a cooperative venture between the Federal Government and the local community.[80] In order to insure some financial support on the local level, and maintain the project's low-rent schedule, the Act required that the community:

(a) raise 10 per cent of the development cost
(b) make local annual contributions to the project.[81]

Officials believed that this requirement would generally be met by complete local tax exemption.[82]

When the Authority made its initial request for Federal funds, it reported that ". . . the city had agreed not to tax the projects . . . and local bankers had indicated a willingness to buy bonds of the Authority to the extent of 10 per cent of the development cost of the projects."[83] Thereupon, the United States Housing Authority entered into Loan and Annual Contributions contracts with the Housing Authority which committed funds to the Pittsburgh program.[84] The local Authority then took preliminary steps towards construction of its first project, Bedford Dwellings.

To finance these steps, the Authority was expected to obtain from the United States Housing Authority advances of funds as they were needed. The United States Housing Authority was required, under the provisions of the Housing Act of 1937, to charge interest on all such advance loans to the local authorities. The rate of interest was determined by means of the "going Federal Rate" of interest, which was defined in the Housing Act of 1937 as

> The rate of interest specified in the most recently issued bonds of the Federal government having a maturity of ten years or more, determined, in the case of loans or annual contributions, respectively, at the date of Presidential approval of the contract pursuant to which such loans or contributions are made.

---

78. See Appendix II, p.
79. Ibid.
80. The low-rent program conducted by the Federal Government through the Public Works Administration had not produced satisfactory results partly as a result of the distrust of local communities, which feared the effects of a Federally directed and controlled program. Thus, the 1937 Housing Act was attempting to overcome this antagonism by providing for local community control.
81. The United States Housing Authority, op. cit., p. 18.
82. Ibid.
83. McGeary, op. cit., p. 11.
84. Other requirements, previously mentioned, had to be met also before final approval was given.

A local authority was required to pay a rate of interest one-half of one per cent above the going Federal rate applicable to its specific contract date. Therefore, the Authority was required to pay an interest rate of three per cent for Federal funds.[85] But "... the local authorities soon learned to save money ... by financing, not only in the construction stage but during the period of initial occurrence, with short-term capital from private sources."[86] The Pittsburgh Authority was able to finance privately its initial cash requirements by the issuance of six-month "temporary loan notes" at a rate of six-tenths of one per cent, instead of financing by use of United States Housing Authority funds, which would have cost approximately two and one-half per cent more.[87]

Under this Act, a local authority could continue its financing on a temporary, short-term basis until 90 per cent of the cost of the development of a project had been spent.[88] At this time, statutory regulations required the permanent financing of the project by the issuance of long-term bonds.[89]

From 1939 until December, 1941, the Authority operated on short-term credit at rates of interest varying from three and one-half tenths of one per cent to six and one-half tenths of one per cent per annum.[90] In December, 1941, the statutory limit had been spent, and the Authority had to finance the projects permanently.[91] Thus the Authority would no longer be paying the low rates of interest from which it had benefited on its short-term financing; instead, the Authority would have to pay the going market rate on at least 10 per cent of the principal amount and a statutory two and one-half per cent to the United States Housing Authority on the remaining balance. At this point, the Comptroller's Office of the Authority conceived of an unusual idea which resulted in a considerable saving to the Authority.[92]

Briefly, the plan was as follows: the original United States Housing loan commitment agreement had covered the construction of Bedford Dwellings and Addison Terrace projects. An additional amount was subsequently authorized for the construction of Wadsworth and Allequippa Terrace so that the initial loan agreement financed of these three projects in the following amounts:

---

85. Office of the Comptroller, Housing Authority of the City of Pittsburgh.
86. McGeary, op. cit., p. 14.
87. When Bedford Dwellings and Addison Terrace projects were financed permanently in December, 1942, the Assistance contracts of these two projects were combined with the contract applicable to Allequippa Terrace into a combination Assistance contract. The going Federal rate applicable at that time was two per cent, and so the Authority had to pay two and one-half per cent instead of three per cent. Housing Authority of the City of Pittsburgh.
88. Housing Authority of the City of Pittsburgh.
89. Ibid.
90. Ibid.
91. Ibid.
92. Comptroller Lester A. Zindel was the chief innovator of this plan; the description of the plan is his account of the events.

| | |
|---|---|
| Addison Terrace . . . . . . . . . . | $ 4,617,215.00 |
| Bedford Dwellings . . . . . . . . . | 2,451,749.00 |
| Allequippa Terrace . . . . . . . . | 9,871,036.00 |
| Total . . . . . . . . . . . . . . . . . | $16,946,000.00 |

When 90 per cent of this amount, or $15,251,000.00 had been spent, the projects had to be financed permanently; this time arrived by December, 1941.

The Authority had already started construction of Arlington Heights and Allegheny Dwellings projects at a combined estimated development cost of $5,425,000.00.[93] The Authority conceived the idea of consolidating the five projects under one Assistance Agreement so that it did not have to finance permanently until 90 per cent of $22,371,000.00 ($16,946,000.00 plus $5,425,000.00), or $20,133,900.00, had been spent. Since the United States Housing Authority approved of this plan, permanent financing on projects Addison Terrace, Bedford Dwellings, and Allequippa Terrace was postponed until late in 1942.[94]

The Authority, therefore, had the use of short-term credit with low interest rates for approximately one additional year. Using an average interest rate of one-half of one per cent (as being approximately the mid-point between 35/100 per cent and 65/100 per cent), the Authority was able to finance for an additional year at a cost of approximately $100,699.50.[95]

The Authority issued the long-term bonds in the principal amount of $16,625,000.00 during December, 1942.[96] In accordance with the provisions of the Housing Act of 1937, this original issue of bonds included two series of bonds. An issue of Series "A" bonds was offered to the public, and the residue of the principal amount being financed was to be sold to the United States Housing Authority in the form of Series "B" bonds. The Authority's bond advertisement in the Daily Bond Buyer, October 1, 1942, provided in part,

> . . . (1) The annual charge of principal and interest of such bonds will absorb as nearly as practicable the sum of $492,000.00 (which is the amount of the Fixed Annual Contribution payable to the Authority by the Federal Public Housing Authority[97] under and subject to the terms and conditions of a contract known as the 'Assistance Contract') in each year except the

93. Arlington Heights project had a total development cost of $3,736,000.00; Allegheny Dwellings, a total development cost of $1,689,000.00. See Appendix II, page
94. Permanent financing was necessitated at this time because the Authority had to split the projects Arlington Heights and Allegheny Dwellings from projects Addison Terrace, Bedford Dwellings, and Allequippa Terrace.
95. An approximate saving of $277,300.00 was achieved since permanent financing of the principal amount would have cost approximately $377,965.00 if sold to private sources at two per cent and the Federal government at the statutory rate of two and one-half per cent.
96. Office of the Comptroller, Housing Authority of the City of Pittsburgh.
97. The United States Housing Authority was superseded by the Federal Public Housing Authority, a constituent agency of the National Housing Agency created in 1942 under the terms of Executive Order 9070.

year 2000 and on the basis that the interest payable on April 1, 1943, will be capitalized; (2) No Series B Bonds shall mature until the April 1 following the last maturity of the Series A bonds, and (3) The amount of bonds in any maturity of Series A bonds in any preceding maturity of Series A bonds, except the maturity of April 1, 1943.

The Series A bonds had been given priority of redemption over the Series B bonds, which were to be sold to the Federal government. In addition, the bond offering advertisement stated that

> The bonds are general obligations of the Authority, secured by a first pledge of the net revenues derived from the operation of the Project on and after the date of the bonds and by a pledge of the annual contributions payable to the Authority by the Federal Public Housing Authority with respect to the project on and after such date under and subject to the terms and conditions of the Assistance Contract.

The Series A bond issue was, in effect, a guaranteed obligation of the United States government, designed for "buyer appeal." Of the principal amount of $16,625,000.00, $9,137,000.00 was purchased by the Mellon Securities Corporation of Pittsburgh with a bid of an average rate of interest of 1.988 per cent as opposed to a 2.04 per cent bid made by a New York syndicate. The balance of $7,488,000.00 was sold to the Federal government at the statutory interest rate of two and one-half per cent.

The Series A bonds were to mature from April 1, 1943, to April 1, 1985, at varying rates of interest, as shown in Table, page 45.[98] Redemption of the Series B bonds was not to begin until after the last Series A bond maturity date, or until the year 1986, since a local authority could retire Series B bonds before their scheduled maturity date only after more than one year's debt service had been earned on the Series A bonds during that particular year. The Schedule of Redemption for the Series B bond issue is shown in Table, page 46.[98]

All of the Series A bonds have been redeemed on their due dates; up to the present, the Authority has not been delinquent in the redemption of any of the Series A bonds nor in any of its debt service obligations. Some of the Series B bonds have been retired even ahead of their maturity dates.[99] This fact seems to indicate that the Authority has adequately met its debt service obligations during the several years of the operation of its projects.

## The Addition of Arlington Heights and Allegheny Dwellings

In January, 1942, construction had started on Allegheny Dwellings; in February, 1942, on Arlington Heights.[100] Unlike their predecessors,

---

98. Housing Authority of the City of Pittsburgh, op. cit., p. 44.
99. See page 46.
100. See Appendix II, page 96.

these two projects were not built for immediate use as low-rent housing projects. By the time construction started on the two projects, the United States had entered World War II, and Pittsburgh, being an industrial center, was gearing itself for maximum effort. Because of Pittsburgh's prominence in steel production, the city anticipated a large influx of war workers who would need adequate housing. Pittsburgh's already serious shortage of decent housing in the peacetime years 1930-1940 was accentuated by the new demands.

A survey in the Pittsburgh area in February, 1942, indicated that usable vacancies in the low and medium-rent ranges were practically non-existent.[101] Out of a total of 180,000 available units, 1.1 per cent were unoccupied and in good condition. Of this percentage, the survey estimated that at least a tenth were above the worker-group income level.

Consequently, Arlington Heights and Allegheny Dwellings projects were completed as housing quarters for defense workers; management of these projects was entrusted to the Authority.[102] These new projects were not financed as the first three had been. The total cost of the projects, amounting to $5,400,825.00 was financed by the occasional insurance of temporary loan notes with varying maturity dates; their rates of interest ranged from 35/100 per cent to 1.83 per cent, depending on market conditions.[103]

The problem of a housing shortage was not strictly a Pittsburgh phenomenon; many other areas across the country felt the pinch of increasing demand on a limited supply. The Federal government attempted to ease the shortage.[104] The first step was the conversion of low-rent projects under construction, such as Pittsburgh's two projects, Arlington Heights and Allegheny Dwellings, into temporary housing for war workers. The workers were required to pay economic rents, subject to the rent ceilings governing privately-owned rental properties.

---

101. Pittsburgh Housing Association. Housing in Pittsburgh, 1941-1942 (Pittsburgh, 1943) p. 6.
102. "By an amendment to the United States Housing Act in 1940 . . . the USHA was authorized to 'develop and administer' projects for defense workers and their families in localities where 'necessary housing would not otherwise be provided.'" McGeary, op. cit., p. 2.
103. Housing Authority of the City of Pittsburgh. This debt was liquidated later with funds from the second long-term bond issue of the Authority, December, 1952.
104. One aspect of this effort was reflected in wartime additions to the available housing supply by the Federal Housing Administration, notably the units added under the provisions of sections 603 and 608 of Title VI, the defense housing amendment to the National Housing Act. Public Law 24, March 28, 1941.

## The Addition of Glen-Hazel Heights

The second step taken by the Federal government was the authorization of the construction of war worker housing under the provisions of the Lanham Act, passed by Congress in the fall of 1940.[105] Under the provisions of this Act, Glen-Hazel Heights project was built in the Hazelwood district of Pittsburgh, its sole wartime purpose being to provide housing for war workers. The ownership of the project was retained by the Federal government although its management was entrusted to the Authority. The total cost of the 999 unit project was $5,388,800.00.[106]

The Federal Works Administration leased Glen-Hazel Heights project to the Authority, but the Federal Public Housing Authority subsequently assumed the role of leasing agent. Under the lease agreement, the Authority acted only in the capacity of management agent. Rents received from the tenants were paid directly to the fiscal agent of the Federal government.[107] The Authority was required to keep separate records for Glen-Hazel Heights; no low-rent housing funds were to be diverted for the maintenance of this project.[108] The Authority was not allowed to make any repairs or improvements on the project, since it was only the managing agent and not the owner. This requirement was to cause serious difficulties for the Authority in subsequent years.

As a consequence of the war-initiated Lanham Act legislation, the Authority had 999 units of rental space added to its rent rolls, but these units were not low-rent. Instead of being occupied by the usual low-income tenants of the Authority, the project was occupied for the duration by war workers who paid rentals based on a rent schedule set by the Federal Public Housing Authority.[109]

## The Addition of Broadhead Manor

In November, 1944, an additional 448 units of space were placed under the management of the Authority by the completion of Broadhead Manor project. The site for Broadhead Manor project was acquired at a cost of $60,690.00. An additional $477,753.52 was spent on direct improvement of the site. Thus a total of $538,443.52 was expended on initial site acquisition and direct development costs.[110]

---

105. Public Law 849, October 14, 1940.
106. See Appendix II, page
107. Ibid.
108. Ibid.
109. The tenants "formed an active Residents' Council which, in 1943, organized a strike against a new rent schedule set by the FPHA." A settlement was worked out subsequently between the tenants, the FPHA, and the Authority. Housing Authority of the City of Pittsburgh, op. cit., p. 20.
110. See Appendix II, page

Broadhead Manor was built by the Federal government but, unlike Glen-Hazel Heights, ownership was vested in the Authority. Provision was made whereby Broadhead Manor would become a low-rent project after the war.

## Housing for the Low-Income Group During World War II

### *The Demolition Program.*

Pittsburgh's public housing program was considerably diverted by the war situation; programs for housing built with the aid of public funds aimed at the creation of additional quarters for war workers. The available supply of public funds could not meet the total demand, and Pittsburgh's housing officials hoped that a large part of the job could be financed by private capital.[111] Not only would units have to be constructed, but already-existing housing would have to be converted into suitable, smaller apartments.

The task ahead was formidable, since Pittsburgh's housing shortage was not war born. As previous data has indicated, a shortage of decent housing had existed in Pittsburgh for a considerable period prior to the war. The war-accentuated demand for housing heightened the severity of the existing situation.

Despite the increased demand and the importance placed on additions to the housing supply, the number of demolitions during the defense period 1940-1941 and the early war year of 1942 illustrated the quantitative and qualitative nature of Pittsburgh's housing problem. The Department of Buildings and Inspections had demolished an average of 733 dwelling units in the period 1934-1937, and the years 1938-1939 had witnessed the clearing of considerable areas for the sites of Bedford Dwellings and the Terrace Villages.[112] As previously mentioned, 1940-1941 reflected defense period conditions, and fewer than 500 dwellings were demolished each year.[113] During 1942, the first full year of war conditions, only 343 dwelling units were demolished.[114] The concentration of demolitions in selected substandard areas illustrated the obvious truth of the statement that ". . . socially and economically depressed areas and the areas of greatest demolition (were) practically identical."[115]

Theoretically, the demolition of a structure resulted in additional

---

111. Pittsburgh Housing Association, Housing in Pittsburgh, 1941-1942, p. 8.
112. In the Bedford Dwellings area, the contracts for tearing down the structures were arranged through the City's Bureau of Building Inspection, which co-operated with the Authority. The Authority itself advertised, however, for bids on the wrecking work at Terrace Village. McGeary, op. cit., p. 23.
113. Pittsburgh Housing Association, Housing in Pittsburgh, 1942-1943 (Pittsburgh, 1944), p. 23.
114. Ibid.
115. Ibid., p. 24.

vacant land; the high demand for urban property should have resulted in utilization of this newly-vacated land. In one sense this did happen, for several areas cleared by demolition were utilized for public improvement projects, notably the Bedford Dwellings and Terrace Village public housing projects. But utilization did not take place to the extent that might have been expected, for the greatest percentage of 1358 building permits issued by the City of Pittsburgh in 1941 were for buildings constructed in peripheral areas of the city, not in substandard housing areas.[116]

As stated, construction of dwellings which did occur in substandard housing areas was confined almost exclusively to the 942 units of public housing built during the period 1939-1942. This relatively small number of new units would not satisfy the demand at that time. The Pittsburgh Housing Association estimated at the close of 1942 that Pittsburgh's public housing supply had ". . . met less than one tenth of the need for such housing."[117]

The war was affecting the slum problem in two very important ways:

(a) First, the tremendous increase of demand on the available housing supply, as indicated by the extremely low vacancy rate of 1.1 per cent, precluded the demolition of all but the very worst dwelling structures.

(b) Secondly, no low-rent projects would be constructed in Pittsburgh prior to the end of the war.

Not only was the city forced to abandon its program of quality improvement through the erection of low-rent public housing projects, but it also had to stop its corollary activity of quantity-reduction of the number of slum dwellings through the demolition program. The number of dwellings demolished dropped from the high of 1069 in 1939 to 273 in 1944 and 174 in 1945.[118]

New housing permits issued during the war years exhibited a similar downward trend with only 189 building permits issued during 1945.[119] According to Pittsburgh Housing Association information, the few demolitions and new housing starts which did take place followed no general trend as to concentration, although few new buildings were erected in demolition areas.[120]

The decline of the city's substandard housing areas was accelerated further by several related factors. First, the war emergency had necessitated a divergence of individual and collective attention from peacetime activities to one common goal of victory. The attainment of this goal demanded a supreme effort from all citizens, and all other

116. Pittsburgh Housing Association, Housing in Pittsburgh, 1941-1942 (Pittsburgh, 1943), p. 24.
117. Ibid., p. 23.
118. Pittsburgh Housing Association, Housing in Pittsburgh, 1945-1946 (Pittsburgh, 1946), p. 14.
119. Ibid.
120. Ibid.

needs became secondary. Pittsburgh's fight against the slum was no exception.

Secondly, the demand for materials and men caused a shortage of labor and supplies in all occupations that could not make some contribution to the war effort. That which was essential and existing was preserved so that the effort necessary to reproduce such structures could be diverted to other essential tasks. Shelter was a prime consideration, and the desire to preserve existing housing made the imaginary line between fit and acceptable housing and unfit and unacceptable housing practically undistinguishable.

Thirdly, all housing was grouped into a common pool; excluding the completion of low-rent projects started before the war and the addition of both permanent and temporary Lanham Act Housing, additions to this pool were almost non-existent during the wartime period.

Fourth, the demand for this relatively fixed supply of housing increased tremendously as the result of two forces: the expected normal increase in population due to the excess of births over deaths during the period 1941-1945, and the unexpected inflex of war workers into a vitally important area.

These forces interacted to produce the inevitable result. The crush of demand on supply forced many individuals and families to "double-up;" the most serious repercussions occurred in the very areas where the quality of housing was the lowest: the substandard or slum housing areas. Therefore, the curtailment of demolitions and the increased demand for housing of any kind made critical Pittsburgh's low-rent housing shortage.

*Rents During World War II.*

One of the most significant economic aspects of the stubstandard housing area is reflected in the rentals paid per occupied unit of living space. The disproportion between rental payment and facilities purchased is reflected in a rental payment which is usually higher than sound reasoning might dictate as a satisfactory amount. Classical economics would define the result as an interaction of supply and demand which, translated into terms of market price, reflects a disproportion between supply and demand; too many people and too few dwelling units. Wartime demand for housing increased this disproportion as the shelter needs of migrant war workers swelled the demand abnormally; shortages of building materials practically prohibited any new residential construction.

As a precaution against the threat of rent inflation, a Rent Section was organized as a voluntary citizen's group by the Consumer Division of the National Defense Advisory Commission. Its main objective was the stabilization of rents through voluntary cooperation.[121] The

121. Pittsburgh Housing Association, Housing in Pittsburgh, 1941-1942 (Pittsburgh, 1943), p. 9.

voluntary aspect of the Committee's actions was short-lived, however, for on April 27, 1942, an eleven-county area around Pittsburgh was declared a "defense-rental area," subject to the rent control provisions of the Price Control Act.[122] March 1, 1942, was set as the date beyond which rents in Pittsburgh could not be increased, except for necessary capital improvements, maintenance, and service.[123]

According to the Maximum Rent Regulation, rents were to remain the same if the services rendered and the accommodations remained the same. Rents were not likely to fall below this maximum, for the excessively high wartime demand would operate to keep them at the maximum level by pushing constantly against the available supply. Therefore, the rent control edict, in effect, declared a rental status quo.

What did this edict mean to the landlord? In the first place, his rental income could not ordinarily advance above the established maximum: secondly, with his gross income fixed, the landlord was faced with a net income that would be depressed by every normal repair he might make, for the rent regulations considered repairs a part of the owner's personal interest in his investment. Repairs, therefore, did not permit an increase in rental. Under more normal economic conditions, the landlord could justify expenditures for repairs and improvements by increasing rentals to any level his judgment indicated. A loss of tenants and a reduction of income might have resulted; nevertheless, the decision remained with the landlord. The war emergency required the relinquishment of this judgment right.

Because of the rent regulations, repairs to properties become virtually non-existent. Some landlords resorted to a practice that was perhaps worse than the cessation of repairs. They sought to increase their net income through provisions of the regulations which allowed an owner to subdivide a single family residence into two or more dwellings, the only stipulation being that he did not charge more for the new units singly than he had charged for the entire premises as of the rent freeze date. Clearly, this was an attractive arrangement for the landlord seeking a means of increasing his income. From the point of view of the tenant, the results were far from satisfactory. The immediate result was an increase in units, but the more permanent result was the overcrowding of dwelling units.

In most instances, the OPA rent control program was effective in the Pittsburgh area, for widespread rises in rents were held in check. Enforcement in the slum areas, however, was somewhat vulnerable.[124]

---

122. Public Law No. 421, 77th Congress, January 30, 1942.
123. Harry E. Pople, "Plight of the Owner Under Rent Control," Journal of Property Management, September, 1943.
124. Pittsburgh Housing Association, Housing in Pittsburgh, 1945-1946 (Pittsburgh, 1947), p. 11.

The rental charged per unit for city apartments in poor condition rose from $15.64 in 1942 to $19.81 in 1945.[125]

The tendency towards "doubling-up," previously noted, and the splitting-up of rental units into smaller sizes aggravated overcrowded conditions. The increases in the number of one-room units were definitely related.[126] In effect, the family living in the substandard area was paying more for less space in 1945 than it had in 1941. Thus the war intensified Pittsburgh's housing problem, particularly in the substandard housing area. Though circumstances dictated the probable rise of "black market" activities, remarkably the spate of increases that might have been expected did not occur.[127]

Unfortunately for tenants, some rentals did advance, particularly in substandard housing areas, which contained a fixed number of available housing units. Advances occurred in spite of both public and private efforts to halt them.

---

125. Ibid.

126. "One considerable increase—in one-room units merits some attention. . . . This increased number of cases, taken in conjunction with the great increase in rent, reflects the severe shortage of accommodations." Pittsburgh Housing Association, Housing in Wartime Pittsburgh, 1943-1945 (Pittsburgh, 1946), p. 21.

127. "The nature of the service sold made chiseling and black-market operations somewhat more difficult than in the case of price controls affecting 'under the counter' commodities." Henry E. Hoagland, Real Estate Principles (New York, 1955), p. 508.

CHAPTER FOUR

# The Post-World War II Era

The coming of peace in 1945 signaled the return to pre-war, peacetime activities. Of course, peace could not be expected on 1940 conditions, for if nothing else had transpired during the war period, four years had certainly passed. Nowhere was the time lapse more pronounced than in those spheres of economic activity that had been curtailed because of war-engendered shortages and restrictions. The national residential housing market felt their full impact.

> "The National Housing Agency estimated that, at the end of 1945, there were nearly two million families who were living doubled-up with other families; 700,000 of this number were married veterans who were forced to double-up during the last quarter of 1945 because they could not obtain separate homes. It was estimated that by the end of 1946 another two million or more families would be in need of housing."[128]

Some easing of the demand for housing might have been expected in Pittsburgh as the army of migrant workers left the area and headed back home. Such was not the case, for many of these temporary residents had decided to become permanent residents. The space vacated by those who did leave was absorbed quickly by other families prefering separate quarters to the ones they had shared with others during the war period. In addition, many new families had been formed, and many husbands and fathers were expected to return home from the armed service.

In 1945 Pittsburgh had an estimated deficit of 9,000 dwelling units for its negro population; this figure, as illustrated by Table I, page 33, did not take into account the increased demand engendered by new family formations. In addition, the number of negro families who were

128. Richard U.Ratcliff, Urban Land Economics (New York,1949), pp. 438-439.

TABLE I

Deficiencies in Housing for Pittsburgh's Negro Population

| Period | | Dwelling Units Gains | Dwelling Units Deficits |
|---|---|---|---|
| 1940 | Disproportion of population and dwellings units inhabited, Census, 1940 . . . . . . . | | 1,045 |
| | Lack of vacancies, deficiencies of facilities, overcrowding, rental disproportions (estimate) . . . . . . . . . . . . . . . . . . . | | 2,325 |
| | Substandardness (estimate) . . . . . . . . | | 3,011 |
| 1940)<br>1945) | Demolitions, 1940-1945, Bureau of Build--ing Inspection . . . . . . . . . . . . . . . . | | 1,904 |
| | Low-rent housing communities erected, 1940-1945, HACP . . . . . . . . . . . . . . | 1,824 | |
| | War-housing communities erected, 1942-1944, HACP . . . . . . . . . . . . . . . . . | 366 | |
| | Private construction . . . . . . . . . . . | 200 | |
| | Population increase, birth over death, migration, 1940-1945 (estimate) . . . . . | | 1,105 |
| | Work migration single units (estimate) . . | | 2,000 |
| | Total . . . . . . . . . . . | | 9,000 |

Source: Pittsburgh Housing Association.

doubled-up could not be predicted with any great degree of accuracy. The figure of 9,000 units did not include deficits for the city's white population; if it had, the resultant estimate would have been substantially higher than that for the negro portion of the city's population.[129] In any event, additional residential housing units were needed for all income levels, but particularly for the low-income family which had suffered from a deficit of available housing space long before World War II.

129. This statement is based on several factors. First, the proportion of Pittsburgh's white population to its negro population was approximately 15 to 1 in 1940, and this proportion probably did not change appreciably in 1945. In addition, the white population did not have much more of an opportunity to move to other quarters than the negro population did during the war. This situation was in opposition to normal conditions when a white family has a much larger potential housing market than the negro family. Statistics are taken from: U.S. Department of Commerce, Metropolitan District Basic Data Sheets, Wash. D.C., 1947, p. 8.

## The Master Plan

In November 1945, the Pittsburgh City Planning Commission submitted to the Mayor and the City Council a publication entitled Pittsburgh, Groundwork and Inventory for the Master Plan.[130] In this report was embodied the status of Pittsburgh's physical area and developments as of that date, together with the Committee's recommendations for the future development of the area.

In general, the report stated that Pittsburgh had reached a crucial point in its development and must plan intelligently for two things: orderly future development and expansion, and the correction of the disorderly development of the past. The prime necessity was the correction of housing conditions, both quantitatively and qualitatively.

Approximately three-quarters of the entire Third Ward of the City of Pittsburgh, contained the Lower Hill District, was designated by the Committee as having the worst possible degree of housing deficiency.[131] Approximately 40 per cent of the structures in this area had been built prior to 1900; 60 per cent were in need of major repairs or private bath, or both; and 14.5 per cent of the dwelling units had 1.5 or more persons per room.[132]

When statistics for the better residential neighborhoods within the city limits were included, the poor condition of Pittsburgh's stock of available housing was still readily apparent. Forty per cent of Pittsburgh's houses had been built prior to 1900; 43.4 per cent were in need of major repairs or private bath, or both; and 9.3 per cent of the dwelling units had 1.5 or more persons per room.[133]

Figure I, page 35, taken from the above report, illustrates graphically the pattern of housing deficiencies throughout the city area. Deficiencies were concentrated in the downtown area, the Northside, and the Southside. Strikingly, however, the deficiency condition stretched from Pittsburgh's Golden Triangle into the Oakland area and along the Allegheny and Monongahela Rivers, well beyond purely business districts into heavily congested industrial and residential areas.

The Committee's proposals and recommendations were not expected to be carried out in full in succeeding years, nor was any degree of rigidity attached to the proposals and recommendations. The recommended plan was intended as a guide that began with an inventory of what actually existed. The report expressed the Committee's opinion that orderly, planned development had to grow, ". . . out of an inventory of physical, social, and financial conditions within the area of the planner's jurisdiction and in relation to the surrounding region.[134]

---

130. Pittsburgh City Planning Commission, Department of City Planning, Pittsburgh, Groundwork and Inventory for the Master Plan. Pittsburgh, 1945.
131. Ibid., p. 64.
132. Ibid., p. 54.
133. Ibid.,
134. Ibid., pp. 8-9.

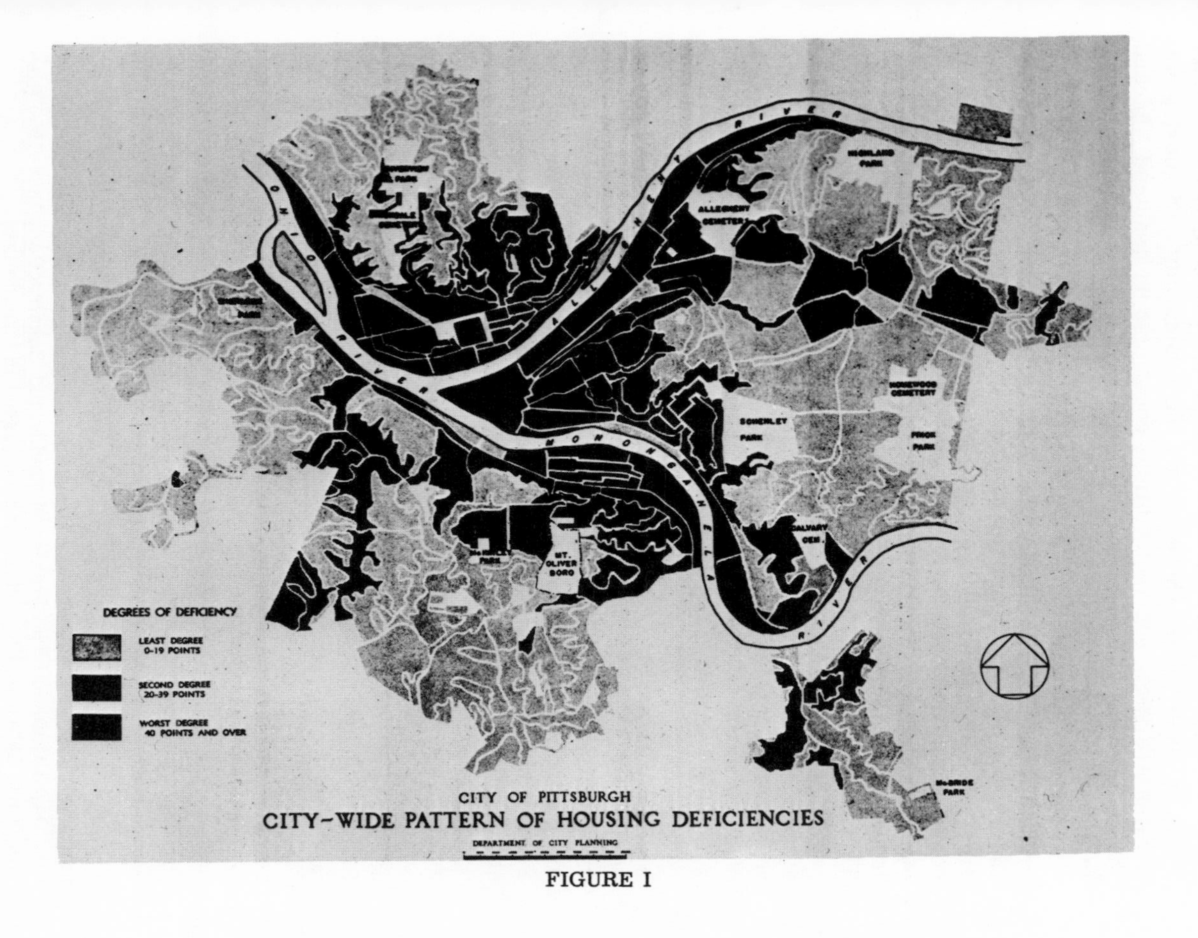
CITY OF PITTSBURGH
CITY-WIDE PATTERN OF HOUSING DEFICIENCIES
DEPARTMENT OF CITY PLANNING
DEGREES OF DEFICIENCY
LEAST DEGREE 0-19 POINTS
SECOND DEGREE 20-39 POINTS
WORST DEGREE 40 POINTS AND OVER
ALLEGHENY RIVER
MONONGAHELA RIVER
OHIO RIVER
HIGHLAND PARK
ALLEGHENY CEMETERY
HOMEWOOD CEMETERY
FRICK PARK
SCHENLEY PARK
CALVARY CEM.
MT. OLIVER BORO
McBRIDE PARK

FIGURE I

If progress were to occur in accord with the desires of Pittsburgh's planners, the city had several obstacles to overcome from the start. First, in those areas where the physical commodity of housing was substandard, poor social conditions could also be assumed. Second, the hilly topography surrounding Pittsburgh did not lend itself to an orderly process of expansion.[135]

Any attempts to fill the housing void depended on the capacity of private enterprise to supply the needed units, for no new authorizations had been made for Federal public low-rent housing assistance since the beginnning of World War II. Restrictions on non-essential construction had been in effect since the fall of 1941; and when construction controls were eliminated in October 1945, commercial and industrial building garnered a disporportionate share of materials.[136] Therefore, the disadvantages enumerated above were coupled with the additional obstacles of legislative restrictions and materials shortages. To remedy the materials situation, Congress reinstituted controls on the construction industry so as to guarantee that a minimum of 50 per cent of all available materials would flow into homes of $10,000.00 or less, or $80.00 or less in rent.[137]

Soon after the reinstitution of construction controls, home-building hesitantly began its post-war spurt to unparalleled heights. For the country as a whole expenditures for new, private, permanent, non-farm, housekeeping dwelling units rose from $720,000,000.00 in 1945 to $3,300,000,000.00 in 1946 to $7,257,000,000.00 in 1949 to $11,525,000,000.00 in 1950.[138] Approximately 85.6 per cent of all such units constructed during the period 1945-1950 were one-family units; the greatest portion was constructed in areas peripheral to urban centers.[139]

In the Pittsburgh area, the results were no less spectacular as new private home construction increased from $42,198,000.00 in 1946 to $56,899,000.00 in 1947 to $136,157,000.00 in 1950.[140] The greatest increases occurred in the suburban areas. In Allegheny County 77.7

135. The Allegheny and Monogahela Rivers were natural barriers to expansion and helped to confine the city within a relatively small land area which was composed largely of hills and valleys with a small, level plateau near the confluence of the rivers.

136. "Apparently, plans for this type of structure were further advanced than in the case of residential building projects, and there was greater willingness to pay whatever prices were necessary in order to permit construction to proceed with dispatch." Ratcliff, op. cit., p. 436.

137. Ibid., p. 438.

138. David M. Blank, The Volume of Residential Construction, 1889-1950 (New York, 1954), p. 69. Prices are expressed in 1954 dollars.

139. Ibid., p. 68.

140. Pittsburgh Housing Association, Housing in Pittsburgh, 1947-1951. (Pittsburgh, 1952), p. 42. The statistics were compiled from the Dodge Corporation Reports.

per cent of the new private dwelling structures were constructed in the period 1946-1950; in the City of Pittsburgh, which contained 44.5 per cent of the total county population, only 22.3 per cent of the private dwelling units were constructed.[141]

This trend was most serious in the case of the city's low-income group. Although appreciable suburban additions were being made to the housing supply which helped to relieve the pressure on the in-city supply, the greatest proportion of the new additions were homes whose selling prices were above the reach of the low-income family. The average expenditure for new, private, permanent, nonfarm housekeeping units had risen from $3,462.00 in 1945 to $8,524.00 in 1950.[142]

Characteristically, the low-income group has much less mobility than the middle-and higher-income groups. Their mobility is restricted by racial barriers (i.e., a greatly reduced potential housing market for negroes as compared to the white, low-income family) and economic barriers. Many low-income families were forced to live in the city center because this location was within walking distance of the place of employment or within a reasonable traveling distance via rapid transportation lines.

The seriousness of the housing problem for the low-income group was compounded by post-war decentralization. Their housing market, already restricted in scope, was not receiving its proportionate share of new additions to the housing supply.

The city's housing problems were, in essence, reducible to two major, interrelated problems. First, was the problem of redeveloping existing residential neighborhoods that had deteriorated into slum areas and of rehabilitating other existing areas that were salvable but in need of extensive repairs. Second, was the problem of adding new dwelling units for families currently residing in the above areas and for families who would live there in the future. Further, these new units would have to be within the economic reach of the low-income family, since the largest percentage of slum families are members of this income classification.[143]

## The United States Housing Act of 1949

Federal assistance for the urban center and its low-income families was provided for in the Housing Act of 1949.[144] In brief, the Act held promise of Federal financial assistance for both conditions of

141. Ibid.
142. Blank, op. cit., p. 70.
143. For example, out of a total of 1097 families interviewed by the Pittsburgh Housing Association in the Lower Hill Redevelopment Area, 802 had incomes below the initial occupancy requirements of the Authority. Pittsburgh Housing Association. Census Survey, Lower Hill Redevelopment Project, Redevelopment Area No. 3. (Pittsburgh, 1953), p. 25. See Appendix I, for the Authority's Eligibility Requirements.
144. Public Law 171. 81st Congress, July 15, 1949.

Pittsburgh's low-rent housing problem. Assistance in the redevelopment of slum areas was offered through the Urban Redevelopment provisions, Title I, of the Housing Act of 1949. Assistance in providing additional low-rent housing units was available through Title III, the public housing section of the Act.

The Housing Act of 1949 authorized financial assistance for an additional 810,000 units of public housing at an annual rate of 135,000 units.[145] Just how quickly the program would get under way depended on, ". . . how quickly the localities (would) complete plans, acquire sites, and get construction underway."[146] Fifty thousand units were expected to be under construction within 12 months after the enactment of the Act.[147]

On August 8, 1949, application forms and instructions were mailed to approximately 500 local housing authorities in 42 states.[148] The principal purpose of these forms was to enable the local authorities to make reservations of specific numbers of public housing units for their respective communities.

In its application, the local authority was required to submit data on the housing supply in its area, including information on the extent of substandard housing. In addition, the community had to submit evidence of an actual existing need for low-rent housing, for the Act required that, "Federal aid be made available only when the local authority demonstrated that there was a definite need for low-rent housing that was not being met by private enterprise."[149]

The authorization of public housing units in the Housing Act of 1949 was the first such authorization since the Housing Act of 1937. Those units of public housing which had been constructed in Pittsburgh under the auspices of the Housing Act of 1937 had fallen far short of effecting any permanent solution to the problem of providing decent low-rent housing for the low-income group. The public housing program, interrupted by World War II and legislative resistance in the immediate post-war years, was reinstated in 1950, and the Housing Authority of the City of Pittsburgh readied plans for the construction of approximately 5,000 units of low-rent public housing.[150]

---

145. The Act provided the President with the discretionary power of increasing the actual number of units to 200,000 units or of reducing it to 50,000 units, depending on economic conditions. Housing and Home Finance Agency, Office of the Administrator, A Handbook of Information on Provisions of the Housing Act of 1949 (Washington, 1949), p. 15.
146. Press Release, Housing and Home Finance Agency, August 8, 1949.
147. Ibid.
148. Ibid.
149. Ibid., p. 3. "The new law requires that a substantial gap be left between the bottom of the market served by private housing and the top of the market served by public housing." Housing and Home Finance Agency. A Handbook of Information on Provisions of the Housing Act of 1949. (Washington, 1949), p. 15.
150. These included Bedford Dwelling Addition, 460 units; St. Clair Village, 1092 units; the North Side project, 3,000 units.

The Housing Act of 1949 was, in essence, an extension by amendments of the principles incorporated in the Housing Act of 1937.[151] The procedure to be followed by a local community was basically the same under both acts. Therefore, a local authority was able to participate in the program by complying with certain step-by-step requirements:[152]

(a) The local authority demonstrates a definite deficiency of public housing in low-rent units.

(b) The local authority then makes application to the Federal government for financial assistance.

(c) The Federal government makes a preliminary loan to cover the cost of surveys and planning of specific housing developments.

(d) Sites are selected and preliminary plans are made. The local authority secures firm estimates of the cost of the housing and its operation.

(e) The local authority secures, from the local governing body, cooperation agreements, which include the governing body's guarantee of tax exemption for a specific number of units and the further guarantee that the residents of the public housing projects will be furnished municipal services in the same manner as other residents of the city.

(f) After preliminary plans are completed and a cooperation agreement is entered into between the Public Housing Administration[153] and the local community, the local housing authority furnishes a development program which contains all the features of the specific proposal. If the Federal government approves, it pledges financial support.

In order to fulfill requirement (a), the Authority submitted to the Public Housing Administration a report which estimated a deficit of 5,000 low-rent housing units.[154] Subsequently, the City of Pittsburgh concurred in this estimate when it completed requirement (e); under an agreement with the Public Housing Administration, the city granted tax exemption privileges to a total of 5,000 new public housing units.[155] Thereupon, the Public Housing Administration entered a permanent

---

151. Under the 1949 Act, the city had to assure the government that safe, decent permanent housing within the income limits of the families being displaced by redevelopment was available or would be provided.

152. The source for this summarization of procedure is A Handbook of Information on Provisions of the Housing Act of 1949, p. 9.

153. The Housing and Home Finance Agency was created in 1947 to succeed the National Housing Agency. The Public Housing Administration was created as one of three constituent agencies. Reorganization Plan No. 3, 80th Congress, July 27, 1947.

154. Office of the Comptroller, Housing Authority of the City of Pittsburgh.

155. The agreement was to run until the 5,000 units had been added. Any new additional units would have to be granted tax privileges under a new, separate agreement. As of January, 1957, the 5,000-unit limit still had not been reached. Ibid.

agreement with the Authority to guarantee Federal financial assistance.

The Authority's initial unit reservations anticipated the addition of almost two times the number of units that had been constructed under the Housing Act of 1937 (excluding Broadhead Manor and Glen-Hazel Heights projects.) In 1950, indications were that the contemplated 5,000 new units of public housing would be occupied quickly by some of the members of an apparently abundant low-income group.

Available statistics indicated the existence of a great deficiency of acceptable units in Pittsburgh's low-rent housing market. Out of a total of 188,949 dwelling units reporting in Pittsburgh for the 1950 United States Census, 76,697 of these were dilapidated and 136,585 of the total number of units reporting had been built in 1919, or earlier.[156]

Theoretically, families of all income groups were competing for the above units, but in actuality, families of relatively low incomes were the prime source of potential renters, for the median rent of 105,239 rental units reported as not dilapidated was $35.83.[157] Pittsburgh's 1950 population of 676,806 had a total of 231,325 families and individuals whose median income was $2,858.00.[158] Of this group, 94,045 had incomes between $2,500.00 and $3,499.00 per year.[159] Only 32,530 of the total group had incomes between $5,000.00 and $9,999.00 per year.[160]

## The Development of Bedford Dwellings Addition and St. Clair Village

Construction started in July, 1951, on Bedford Dwellings Addition; in November of the same year construction started on St. Clair Village.

Bedford Dwellings Addition is an extension of the Authority's first low-rent project, Bedford Dwellings. Located on a site totaling 19.5 acres, the project provides an additional 460 units, 220 units added on one side of Bedford Dwellings and 240 units on the other.[161] The total site area was acquired for $852,204.48; an additional $741,914.10 was spent for site improvements. Thus a total investment of $1,593,917.58 was required to make the sites ready for use.[162]

156. U.S. Bureau of the Census. U.S. Census of Population: 1950. Vol. III, Census Tract Statistics, Chapter 43. (Washington, 1952) p. 92.
157. Ibid.
158. Ibid., p. 8.
159. Ibid.
160. Ibid.
161. The Housing Authority of the City of Pittsburgh, "Public Housing in Pittsburgh, 1938-1953," A Report to the People (Pittsburgh, 1953), p. 21.
162. See Appendix II, page 160. In actual practice, some of the site development was not completed until after the buildings had been completed. The separation of land and buildings has been done for illustrative purposes.

This location was chosen for the first post-war project of the Authority because of several factors. First, the proximity of its location to the original Bedford Dwellings afforded the many advantages of continuity of operation: merely extending the operational and managerial controls over a wider geographic area and a larger number of units and tenants.[163] Second, the site area contained mainly substandard dwelling units and a few "lower-use" business enterprises. Third, the elevation afforded natural advantages, for the homes were to be located high above the noise and smoke of Pittsburgh's industrial plants. The Authority consistently tried to locate its projects on sites of high elevation.

The location of St. Clair Village differs sharply from the location of any other of the Authority's low-rent projects, for this project is not located within Pittsburgh's urban center, nor in highly congested industrial areas of the city's periphery. The project does have one characteristic common to the other low-rent projects, however, for the Authority chose a site of high elevation on which to locate St. Clair Village. Undoubtedly, cost factors had some part in this preference for hilly, largely undeveloped sites.

Initial site acquisition costs totaled $562,109.23, and an additional $1,783,730.32 was spent on improving the site.[164] The purchase price reflects the lower land value in the peripheral area as well as the condition of the site at the time of purchase. The fact that over three times the initial acquisition cost was spent on site improvement indicates that the site was not readily adaptable to any large-scale development, such as St. Clair Village.

> The site originally consisted of two hills separated by a ravine, with the entire area of 107 acres surrounded on three sides by steep, unbuildable slopes. After an extensive grading operation, including cuts of 35 feet and the moving of 530,000 cubic yards of earth, this semi-rural site has been converted into a well-planned community of 1089 homes.[165]

## Firts Issue of New Housing Authority Bonds[166]

The first postwar permanent financing of the Authority was undertaken for two purposes. First, the construction of Arlington Heights

163. The Authority treats Bedford Dwellings and the Addition as one and the same project for its own accounting and operational purposes, but it must separate them when submitting reports to the Regional Public Housing Authority Office. Office of the Comptroller, Housing Authority of the City of Pittsburgh.
164. See Appendix II, page
165. A Report to the People, p. 22.
166. This issue of bonds was called "New Housing Authority Bonds" to distinguish them from the pre-war long-term bond issues (called, "Housing Authority Bonds"). Prior to offering the bond issue for public bid and sale, the Federal government makes a definite commitment to take a

and Allegheny Dwelling projects had been financed by the Authority through Federal Temporary Loan Notes. Because World War II was in progress at the time of their completion, the projects were not permanently financed as they would have been under peace-time conditions. As a result, the short-term debt incurred by the Authority through construction of these projects was still outstanding in December 1952. Secondly, the first post-war project of the Authority, Bedford Dwellings Addition, had reached the stage in its development when the Law required the local authority to finance the debt permanently.[167]

Circumstances dictated the issuance of long-term bonds on Bedford Dwellings Addition. Arlington Heights and Allegheny Dwellings projects, however, were to be permanently financed. Part of the proceeds of the bond sale was to be used to retire, at least partially, the amount of existing short-term debt on the two projects.[168]

Subsequently, the Authority offered for sale its first issue of New Housing Authority Bonds in the principal amount of $8,210,000.00 at a level interest rate of 2-3/8 per cent.

### Second Issue of New Housing Authority Bonds

On December 29, 1954, the Authority submitted proposal forms covering the sale of its second long-term New Housing Authority Bond issue to various bond-purchasing syndicates.[169] Details of the proposed issue appeared in the Notice of Sale of the Authority in the December 18, 1954, issue of the Daily Bond Buyer. The proposal contained several schedules of annual maturities at various interest rates ranging from 2-1/8 per cent to 2-7/8 per cent in 1/8 of one per cent multiples.[170]

When bids were opened at the office of the Authority on January 11, 1955, the entire issue was bought by a syndicate for an interest rate of 2-1/4 per cent.

---

certain percentage of the issue. Theoretically, the amount subscribed for is the deficiency which results after public demand has bought its share of the bond issue. This deficiency is taken up by the Federal government through a permanent note issued by the Authority in favor of the Federal government for the full amount; this permanent note serves as the collateral for the issuance of Temporary loan notes.

167. This limit was reached when 90 per cent of the total amount of the estimated development cost of the project had been spent.

168. "Any permanent financing is used to liquidate if not in full then part of any form of outstanding indebtedness, be it temporary notes, PHA permanent notes and/or PHA Advance Notes." L. A. Zindel, Comptroller, Housing Authority of the City of Pittsburgh, in a letter to the author, dated February 13, 1957.

169. Letter of Transmittal, Housing Authority of the City of Pittsburgh, December 29, 1954.

170. Ibid.

The bond issue had as one of its purposes the permanent financing of the debt incurred through construction of St. Clair Village project. It was also intended to finance on a permanent basis Broadhead Manor, which was to be converted shortly into a low-rent project. Since the project was to be a full-fledged member of Pittsburgh's public housing community, its construction cost, financed by short-term Federal funds, was to be refinanced on a long-term, permanent basis.

The second issue of New Housing Authority bonds completed the permanent financing of Pittsburgh's existing low-rent public housing properties. The future construction of low-rent communities will necessitate further long-term bond issues, but any such plan would be subject to the contingencies of legislative attitude towards the public housing program.[171]

## The Addition of Broadhead Manor and Glen-Hazel Heights

Broadhead Manor and Glen-Hazel Heights were built during World War II to serve as homes for war workers. The projects were not considered as low-rent public housing, even though they were operated by the Authority, for the rents charged did not conform to the low-rent schedules of the Authority. Rather, rentals in these properties were comparable to those for privately-owned and operated rental properties; their rent levels were subject to the same rent control regulations as privately-owned rental housing.

Broadhead Manor was built by the Federal government with ownership vested in the Authority, with the understanding that the project would become a low-rent project some time after the war. Accordingly, Broadhead Manor did become a low-rent community on February 1, 1953, subject to all the operating regulations and tenancy requirements of the other permanent public housing projects.

Glen-Hazel Heights was built under provisions of the wartime Lanham Act. When World War II ended, the Federal government was faced with the problem of divesting itself of ownership of the Lanham Act projects. The Housing and Home Finance Agency was given the responsibility of disposing of these housing units acquired by the government.[172] Pending disposal, the Public Housing Authority operated these projects as rental properties for the Housing and Home Finance Agency.[173]

Accordingly, the Pittsburgh Authority continued to operate Glen-Hazel Heights in the post-war period. Efforts were made to sell the projects to the tenants as a cooperative, but these were not success-

---

171. Presently the Authority has three additional projects under consideration and is planning to issue its third New Housing Authority bond series in the spring of 1957.
172. Paul F. Wendt, The Role of the Federal Government in Housing (Washington, 1956), p. 15.
173. Ibid.

ful. Finally, the government decided to sell Glen-Hazel Heights to the Authority for use as a low-rent project, and the Authority agreed to pay all net income from the project to the Federal government for a period of forty years.[174]

The acquisition of the project was not the bonanza one might have expected. As previously stated, the Authority managed the project for the Federal government prior to acquiring ownership. Under the terms of its management contract, the Authority could not make any improvements to the project, for the Federal government had sole responsibility for making repairs. Unfortunately, the Federal government did not make the repairs and improvements necessary for proper project maintenance and preservation.[175] In addition, the tenants showed no desire to maintain their respective quarters and communal property in good condition.

Therefore, the Authority was faced with the problem of long overdue repairs and replacements which were to be made only out of the project's residual receipts. Obviously, the necessary repairs and replacements could be made only piecemeal over a period of years. In the meantime, deteriorations could be expected to continue, and the unattractive physical appearance of the project would ultimately militate against full occupancy.

---

174. Office of the Comptroller, Housing Authority of the City of Pittsburgh.

175. The need for making repairs was increased by the poor quality of materials used in the construction of Glen-Hazel Heights. Many wartime substitute materials were used; most of these did not measure up to city building requirements.

CHAPTER FIVE

# Total Pittsburgh Investment in Public Housing

With the completion of Bedford Dwellings Addition and St. Clair Village and the conversion of Broadhead Manor and Glen-Hazel Heights to low-rent status, the present complement of 7,011 units of the Authority was complete.

## Value of Land, Structures, and Equipment

The total investment in the land, structures and equipment of Pittsburgh's public housing projects is detailed in Appendix III. The summary of investment, per project, is as follows:

| | |
|---|---|
| PA-1-1 | $ 4,708,584.26 |
| PA-1-2 | 2,505,015.46 |
| PA-1-3 | 10,091,509.91 |
| PA-1-4 | 3,716,439.29 |
| PA-1-5 | 1,724,665.01 |
| PA-1-6 | 2,704,260.03 |
| PA-1-7 | 13,000,078.06 |
| PA-1-8 | 6,410,792.73 |
| PA-1-10 | 5,269,469.54 |
| Total | $50,130,814.35 |

This total of approximately 50 million dollars includes expenditures of $16,128,018.35 for land (including initial acquisition and development costs), $32,756,537.41 for structures, and $1,246,258.49 for equipment.

### Long-Term Indebtedness[176]

The long-term bonds of the Authority were issued in the following principal amounts:

| | | |
|---|---|---|
| 1st Housing Authority Bonds . . . . . . . | | $16,946,000.00 |
| Series A . . . . . | $9,137,000.00 | |
| Series B . . . . . | 7,809,000.00 | |
| 1st New Housing Authority Bonds . . . . | | 8,210,000.00 |
| 2nd New Housing Authority Bonds . . . . | | 15,715,000.00 |
| Total | | $40,871,000.00 |

Bonds have been retired on schedule as they have matured so that as of December 31, 1955, the long-term indebtedness of the Authority had been reduced by bond retirement, as follows:

| | | |
|---|---|---|
| 1st Housing Authority Bonds . . . . . . . | | $ 2,290,000.00 |
| Series A . . . . . | $2,120,000.00 | |
| Series B . . . . . | 170,000.00 | |
| 1st and 2nd New Housing Authority Bonds . . . . . . . . . . . . . | | 300,000.00 |
| Total | | $ 2,590,000.00 |

Therefore, the Authority's outstanding long-term bonded debt had been reduced to $38,281,000.00 by December 31, 1955.

In addition to this outstanding long-term indebtedness, the Authority is liable for another long-term debt in the amount of $4,117,821.00 which it incurred by virtue of its purchase of Glen-Hazel Heights project from the Federal Government.

Total long-term debt, as of December 31, 1955, was, therefore, $42,398,821.00.

### Cumulative Federal Contributions[177]

The Federal government makes subsidy payments on behalf of a project if it operates at a deficit; that is, if receipts are exceeded by disbursements, the Federal government will then make a subsidy contribution equal to the deficit. The Federal government expects these deficit payments plus the amount of the original subsidy, over the life of a project, to equal twice the amount of a local community's contribution through tax exemption granted to the projects.[178]

176. Long-term indebtedness statistics are taken from the project balance sheets as detailed in Appendix III.
177. Cumulative Federal Contributions Statistics are taken from the project balance sheets. (See Appendix III.)
178. Housing and Home Finance Agency, Office of the Administrator, "The Local Contribution," A Handbook of Information on Provisions of the Housing Act of 1949 (Washington, 1949), p. 13.

When the Federal government enters into an Annual Assistance Contract, it guarantees to make subsidy payments up to some set maximum. The initial assistance contract of the Authority, covering its first three projects, Addison Terrace, Bedford Dwellings and Allequippa Terrace, provided for a maximum subsidy payment per year of one per cent higher than the same "going Federal rate" on which the borrowing rate of the Authority was determined. This percentage rate was to be applied to the total project development cost. Since the applicable Federal rate was two per cent, the Authority could claim an annual subsidy of three per cent of the total project development cost.

The second Annual Contributions Contract, covering the operation of projects Arlington Heights, Allegheny Dwellings, Broadhead Manor, St. Clair Village, and Bedford Dwellings Addition, provides for a maximum subsidy payment equal to 5-1/8 per cent per annum of the total development cost until June 30, 1954, and 4-7/8 per cent per annum thereafter.[179]

Glen-Hazel project, PA-1-10, does not have an Annual Contributions Contract. Under the terms of the agreement between the Authority and the Federal Government, the purchase price of the project was its net income for a forty year period; consequently, no debt service and/or Annual Contributions were necessary.

> In setting up the cost accounts at the time of conveying this project, the off-setting credit was 'Unamortized Administration Contract.' This latter account will be proportionately reduced over the (term of the contract)—the reduction is represented by charges to 'Cumulative PHA Contributions' and will therefore eventually amortize the value at time of conveyance, regardless of the amount of residual receipts paid to the Government.[180]

Subsidy payments on behalf of projects Addison Terrace, Bedford Dwellings, and Allequippa Terrace are made under the terms of Annual Contributions Contract No. HAph 1031. Payments made on behalf of projects Arlington Heights, Allegheny Dwellings, Broadhead Manor, St. Clair Village, and Bedford Dwellings Addition are governed by Annual Contributions Contract No. NY-197. The amortization of the cost of Glen-Hazel Heights project, which, in effect, is a Federal subsidy contribution, is governed under the terms of Annual Contributions Contract No. (PA-36101)D1006.

By December 31, 1955, total subsidy contributions made under each of these three Annual Contributions Contracts totaled:

179. Initially, projects PA-1-4, 1-5, and 1-8 were covered under one Assistance Contract, and projects PA-1-6 and 1-7 were covered under another contract. Both of these contracts were subsequently merged into one; the rates applicable to this combination contract have been amended from time to time. The above rates became applicable under the amendment dated December 15, 1953.

180. L. A. Zindel, Comptroller, Housing Authority of the City of Pittsburgh, in a letter to the author dated February 13, 1957.

| | |
|---|---|
| HAph 1031 . . . . . . . . . . . . . . . . . | $1,777,634.90 |
| NY-197 . . . . . . . . . . . . . . . . . . . | 1,860,901.98 |
| (PA-36101)D1006 . . . . . . . . . . . . . | 216,727.44 |
| Total . . . . . . . . . . . | $3,855,264.32 |

Technically, the Authority could have claimed subsidy payments greatly in excess of the amounts actually received. In this regard, one further factor must be emphasized: future subsidy payments can be considerably higher than they have been if economic or social conditions should adversely affect the income operations of the projects.

These annual subsidy payments constitute a contribution by the Federal government and, in a technical sense, do not represent local contributions to the projects. In actual practice, however, the initial donors of all Federal funds are local taxpayers. Thus at least a percentage of public housing subsidy payments made to local authorities are local contributions; exactly what percentage local funds would contribute to the total paid to the local Authority is impossible to determine. Regardless of the specific percentage involved, the present method of subsidy payment represents one manner in which local taxpayers contribute to the operation of public housing projects in their respective communities.

### The Payment-In-Lieu of Taxes

In addition to the aforementioned method of subsidy, local residents make another contribution to their community's public housing projects through the medium of tax-exemption for the public housing projects.

The tax laws of the State of Pennsylvania provide for a tax on all real property, with certain exclusions such as the property of religious organizations. The revenue from these taxes is used, in part, for the purchase and provision of certain services which the community requires for its orderly and healthy existence. Among these services would be included fire and police protection, maintenance of the school system, road maintenance, garbage collection, maintenance of the municipal government, and health services. The contribution made by each home and land owner to the various taxing bodies purchases for him the above services.

Theoretically, each land owner pays his proportionate share of the cost of these services by means of a system of tax assessment. The real property of the community is assessed at a certain percentage of its appraised value (Pittsburgh averages about 50 per cent). The tax millages levied by the counties, municipalities, and school districts are applied to this assessed value, and the tax revenue is determined accordingly. The revenue derived is then disbursed by the taxing bodies (city, school, and county).

The Authority does not make tax payments based on assessed valuations. A substitute though not comparable payment is termed "In Lieu of Taxes." It is the Authority's complete contribution to the cost of the municipal and other services.

The payment-in-lieu of taxes is determined on the basis of the rental income of the projects, less the cost of utilities. The figure remaining after the subtraction of the cost of utilities is called the "Shelter Rent." A percentage of the shelter rent is paid to the taxing bodies. The Housing Act of 1949 provides for the following:

> The locality is required to make a contribution to keeping rents low in the form of exemption from all real and personal property taxes . . . . So that Public Housing projects shall bear a share of the cost of such municipal services as schools and streets, the law permits local authorities to make payments-in-lieu of taxes up to 10 per cent of the shelter rents charged in the projects.[181]

The payment-in-lieu can never be as great as the tax on assessed valuation would be. It could be reduced at the discretion of the Authority to only a token payment. The difference between the in-lieu payments and actual taxes is the contribution that the local community makes to the housing projects in an effort to maintain the low rental level. The local government must make this concession if it desires to have public housing.

Because of this tax exemption privilege, the average taxpayer residing in an area that has public housing pays for the projects in two ways:

(a) by income and other tax payments to the Federal government and ultimate disbursement of these taxes to the local housing authorities as subsidy payments;

(b) by the vehicle of the payment-in-lieu of taxes which provides less municipal revenue per family than private housing in like locations.

In an effort to present a comparison between the payments-in-lieu of taxes by families living in Pittsburgh's public housing projects and the actual real property tax paid by or for families living in private housing in the immediate areas, the writer undertook to establish a payment per family in four different areas. Three of these are areas of privately owned houses located in the Third and Fifth Wards of the City of Pittsburgh in or adjacent to areas recently condemned as substandard. The fourth area includes the nine public housing projects of the Housing Authority of the City of Pittsburgh. Each substandard area is presented individually and then compared with this public housing area.

In the writer's opinion, the major point of disagreement on public housing is the problem of cost. Those opposed to subsidized housing cite the cost of the program as an imposition on the tax-paying public

---

181. Housing and Home Finance Agency, op. cit., p. 13.

and too big a burden for it to bear. Those in favor of subsidized housing recognize this problem and counter the criticism by saying that no price is too great if it will buy decent housing for the low income families. Two examples of adverse criticism follows:

> Since the beginning of the year 1946, the realtors and builders of America have built 6,800,000 new residential units at an average cost of $9,100.00. The 'Public Housers' during the same period built only 233,000 new residential units at an average cost of $11,600.00 per unit.[182]

> I can comprehend the simple things and I know that each tenement dwelling constructed in the public housing program costs upwards of $12,000.00. If there are 200,000 units of this barrack housing in the country, the base cost is already about two and one half billion without adding on the accumulated costs of operation.[183]

Those in favor of subsidized housing answer as follows:

> We in the Pittsburgh Housing Association do not give a continental for public housing as such—nor for any other particular kind of housing as such . . . . We just want to see all Americans well sheltered. There are a number of families in every community who can get good housing only with such subsidies as the rest of us are willing to grant them until they can get on their own feet. Since 1937, we have subsidized them through public housing.[184]

> Here you have my case for public housing . . . . Its' costs are negligible, far outweighed in size by any other number of government subsidies.[185]

Each side feels fully justified in its reasoning. The writer's findings in this portion of the study give full support to neither side, i.e., all public housing or no public housing; furthermore, the writer does not take issue with such general statements. Such specific statements as the following are more important.

> Although less than full taxes would be on new privately owned buildings, these payments (in-lieu-of taxes) are many times in excess of the amounts formerly paid by the slum or blighted properties replaced by the Authority communities. Again, compared to the 'billed' taxes on many existing slum properties, our payments (averaging in 1952 about $40.00 per family housed in low-rent communities) are considerably greater.[186]

The validity of this statement will be discussed in a following section, for on the basis of statistics revealed by the study, it is definitely misleading.

182. From an address by Charles B. Shattuck, Past President, National Association of Real Estate Boards, to the Greater Pittsburgh Board of Realtors, February, 1953.
183. Morgan L. Fitch, "A Realtor Says No to Public Housing," National Real Estate and Building Journal, March, 1954, 55:23.
184. Bryn J. Hovde, "Editorial," Housing News, Vol. 1, October, 1953.
185. Charles E. Slusser, "The Commissioner's Case for Public Housing," National Real Estate and Building Journal, March, 1954, 55:30.
186. Housing Authority of the City of Pittsburgh, op. cit., p. 30.

*The Lower Hill Survey.*

The first survey is centered in the Third Ward of the City of Pittsburgh. This area furnishes an excellent example of a decayed and blighted neighborhood. It is so far downhill that the area is scheduled for redevelopment; that is, the existing structures are to be torn down and new buildings constructed (including a new civic light opera and high-rental apartment buildings). The Lower Hill area, therefore, seems representative of slums at their worst; consequently, tax paid on properties in this area is revenue from slum dwelling families.

Population figures for this survey were taken from a survey of the Lower Hill area made by the Pittsburgh Housing Association for the Pittsburgh Housing Authority. The survey, conducted during the period from December 1953 to February 1953, was made to determine the size and complexity of the Lower Hill population in anticipation of relocating this population in other areas. The survey covers approximately 1,800 families.

The territorial limits of the writer's survey and the location of specific parcels included are detailed in the appendices, Figure VI, page 97.

The assessment figures for this area were taken from the appraisal survey conducted by Harold F. Burnworth and Meyer H. Sachs in July 1950 for the Urban Redevelopment Authority of the City of Pittsburgh. A spot check found the assessments substantially unchanged.

Tax millages for 1955 were applied to the corresponding assessment figures. The millage figures were:

(1) City[187]
- a. Land .032
- b. Building .016

(2) School .01175

(3) County .010375

The tax assessments, multiplied by the above millages, equal the revenue from each property paid to the various taxing bodies.

The remaining tax revenue derived from single persons was deducted from the total tax revenue of each parcel that housed single persons. Single persons were not counted as family units because they are not eligible for public housing. Therefore, if a parcel containing eight rooms and a single person occupied one of these rooms, i.e., one-eighth of the room space, the tax shares of this person was assumed to be one-eighth of the total. This part was deducted, leaving seven-eighths to be apportioned among the occupant families. This distribution per family is shown in Figure II, page 52 and Table II, page 56.

187. Pittsburgh, unlike many United States cities, has a separate millage for land and buildings. For a more detailed discussion of Pittsburgh's tax system, see The City Real Estate Tax in Pittsburgh, by J. P. Watson, Bureau of Business Research, University of Pittsburgh, 1934.

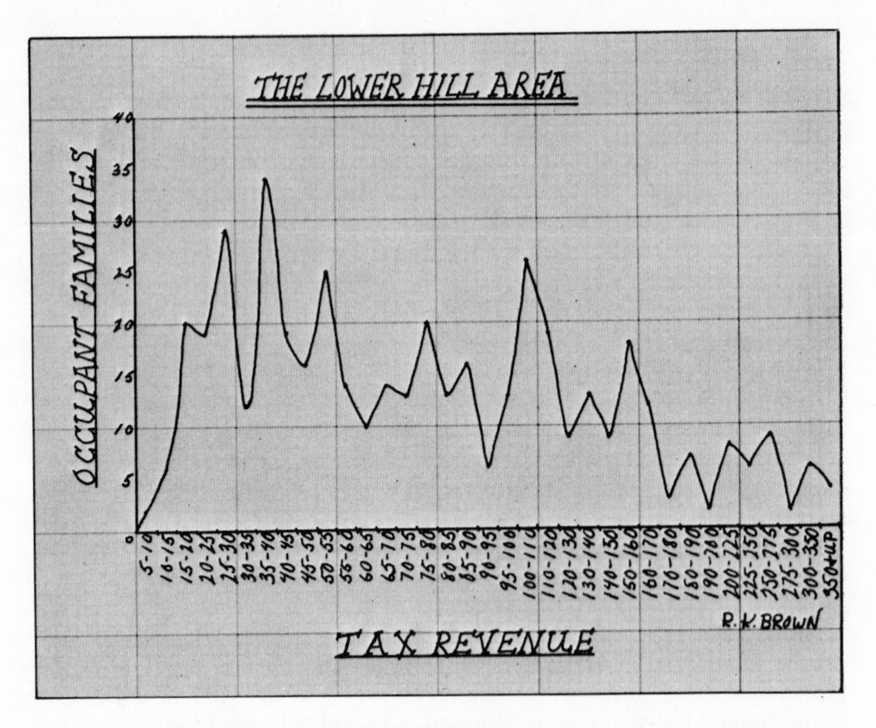


FIGURE II

The tax revenues per occupant family were then totaled, and the resulting figure was then divided by the number of families included in the survey area. Mean averages were brought up by a relatively small number of large individual cases.

The survey area covers 179 parcels of property and 457 family units. The total of the tax revenue payments per occupant family is $41,696.63. This sum, divided by the number of families, is $91.22, which represents an average tax revenue payment per occupant family for the Lower Hill area.

*The Terrace Village Area and Bedford Dwellings Area Surveys.*

The slum or substandard areas adjacent to Terrace Village and Bedford Dwellings projects were chosen for this study because of their proximity to these two finished public housing projects. The writer has been advised that these areas are comparable to what are now considered as substandard areas. Results from surveys of these areas, therefore, would be reasonable figures in comparison with figures from the public housing projects.

The territorial limits of each survey are indicated in Figures VII and VIII, pages 98 and 99. The location of each dwelling unit used in the two surveys is also indicated on these drawings.

The population statistics used in these two surveys were obtained by personal interviews conducted in the areas. A sample of the questionnaire is shown below:

Name . . . . . . . . . . . . . . . . . . . . . . . . . . . . . .

Address . . . . . . . . . . . . . . . . . . . . . . . . . . . .

Number of occupied rooms . . . . . . . . . . . . . . . . . .

Family units . . . . . . . . . . . . . . . . . . . . . . . . . .

Number of rooms occupied by each family . . . . . . . . . .

The property assessments pertaining to each parcel in each survey were obtained in the Recorder of Deeds Office, County Office Building, Pittsburgh, Pennsylvania. Assessments included in the two survey areas are entered in the Fifth Ward Books of the City of Pittsburgh, Parts one and two.

Tax revenues were calculated in the same manner as those in the Lower Hill Survey. The number of occupant families and their proportionate tax payments were also determined in the same manner, as previously described.

The Terrace Village Area Survey includes 43 parcels of property and 85 occupant families. The total of the tax revenues is $4,917.14. This figure, divided by the total number of occupant families included in the survey, results in an average tax payment per occupant family of $56.87. The distribution per family is shown in Figure III, page 54 and Table II, page 56.

The survey of the Bedford Dwellings Area includes 41 dwellings. These units are occupied by 57 families making a total tax payment of $2,567.77. This figure, divided by the number of families included in the survey, reflects an average tax revenue payment of $45.21. The distribution per family is shown in Figure IV, page 55 and Table II, page 56.

*The Public Housing Area Survey.*

This survey includes nine of the public housing projects under the control and jurisdiction of the Housing Authority of the City of Pittsburgh. They are as follows:

PA-1-1 . . . . . . . . . . . . Addison Terrace
PA-1-2 . . . . . . . . . . . . Bedford Dwellings
PA-1-3 . . . . . . . . . . . . Wadsworth-Allequippa Terrace
PA-1-4 . . . . . . . . . . . . Arlington Heights
PA-1-5 . . . . . . . . . . . . Allegheny Dwellings
PA-1-6 . . . . . . . . . . . . Broadhead Manor
PA-1-7 . . . . . . . . . . . . St. Clair Village
PA-1-8 . . . . . . . . . . . . Bedford Dwellings Addition
PA-1-10 . . . . . . . . . . . Glen-Hazel Heights

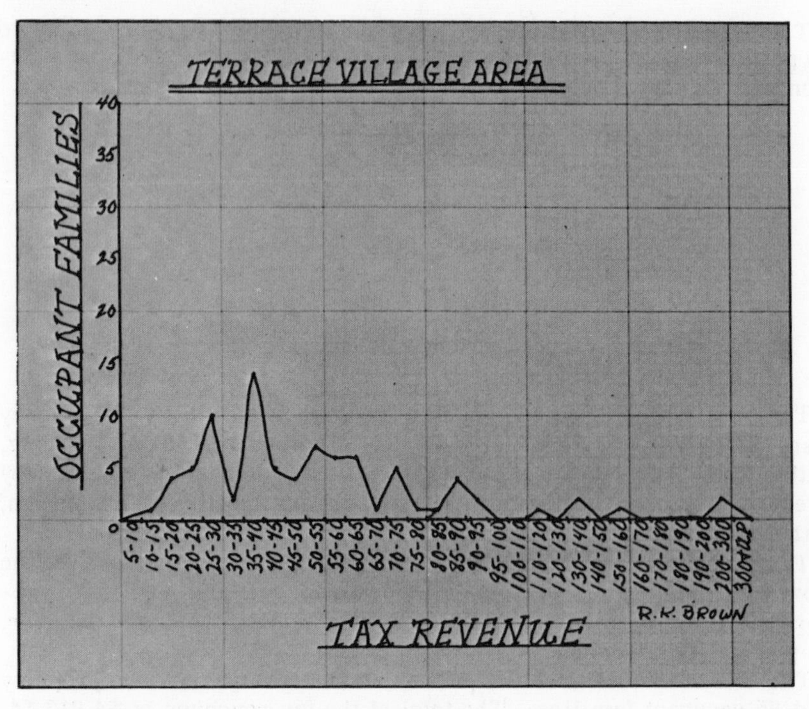


FIGURE III

The total of the payments-in-lieu of taxes by the above mentioned nine projects was $274,168.37 for the year 1955. The number of occupied units and, hence, occupant families in these projects is 7,011. The total amount of the payments-in-lieu of taxes, divided by the total number of occupied units makes an average payment per occupant family of $3.26 per month, or $39.09 per year.

*The Surveys Combined.*

The results of the four survey areas expressed in terms of a mean average payment per occupant family per year are as follows:

1. Lower Hill Survey . . . . . . . . . . . . . . . . . . . . . $91.22
2. Terrace Village Area Survey . . . . . . . . . . . . . 56.67
3. Bedford Dwellings Area Survey . . . . . . . . . . . 45.21
4. Public Housing Area Survey . . . . . . . . . . . . 39.09

The tax payments per occupant family per year expressed in terms of a medain unit (the middle unit with 50 per cent of the sample above it and 50 per cent below it) are as follows:

1. Lower Hill Survey . . . . . . . . . . . . . . . . . . $70-75
2. Terrace Village Area Survey . . . . . . . . . . . 45-50
3. Bedford Dwellings Area Survey . . . . . . . . . 35-40

The tax payments per occupant family per year expressed in terms of a mode unit (the most prevalent unit) are as follows:

1. Lower Hill Survey . . . . . . . . . . . . . . . . . . $35-40
2. Terrace Village Survey . . . . . . . . . . . . . . 35-40
3. Bedford Dwellings Survey . . . . . . . . . . . . 20-35

The three survey areas combined results in the following average units are:

1. Mean Average . . . . . . . . . . . . . . . . . . . . . $81-94
2. Median Average . . . . . . . . . . . . . . . . . . . 55-60
3. Mode Average . . . . . . . . . . . . . . . . . . . . 35-40

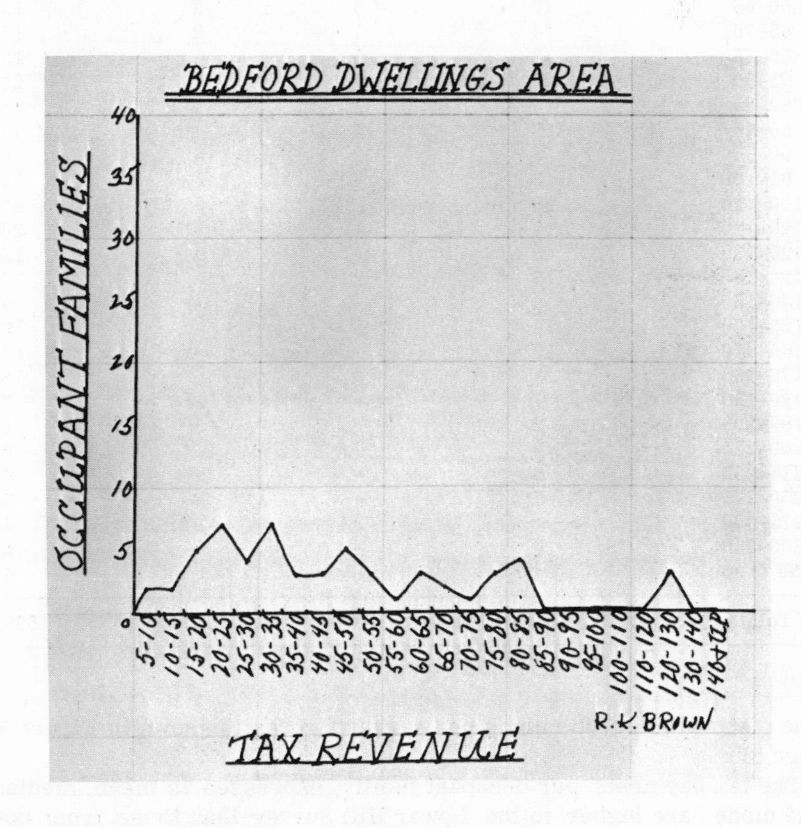


FIGURE IV

TABLE II

Distribution of Tax Revenue Payments
Among Occupant Families

| Tax Revenue | Occupant Families | | | Total |
|---|---|---|---|---|
| | Lower Hill | Terrace Village | Bedford Dwellings | |
| $ 5-10 | 2 | - | 2 | 4 |
| 10-15 | 11 | 1 | 4 | 16 |
| 15-20 | 20 | 4 | 4 | 29 |
| 20-25 | 19 | 5 | 7 | 31 |
| 25-30 | 29 | 10 | 4 | 13 |
| 30-35 | 12 | 2 | 7 | 21 |
| 35-40 | 34 | 14 | 3 | 51 |
| 40-45 | 19 | 5 | 3 | 27 |
| 45-50 | 16 | 4 | 5 | 25 |
| 50-55 | 25 | 7 | 3 | 35 |
| 55-60 | 14 | 6 | 1 | 21 |
| 60-65 | 10 | 6 | 3 | 19 |
| 65-70 | 14 | 1 | 2 | 17 |
| 70-75 | 13 | 5 | 1 | 19 |
| 75-80 | 20 | 1 | 3 | 24 |
| 80-85 | 13 | 1 | 4 | 18 |
| 85-90 | 16 | 4 | - | 20 |
| 90-95 | 6 | 2 | - | 8 |
| 95-100 | 13 | - | - | 13 |
| 100-110 | 26 | - | - | 26 |
| 110-120 | 19 | 1 | - | 20 |
| 120-130 | 9 | - | 3 | 12 |
| 130-140 | 13 | 2 | - | 15 |
| 140-150 | 9 | - | - | 9 |
| 150-160 | 18 | 1 | - | 19 |
| 160-170 | 12 | - | - | 12 |
| 170-180 | 3 | - | - | 3 |
| 180-190 | 7 | - | - | 7 |
| 190-200 | 2 | - | - | 2 |
| 200-225 | 8 | - | - | 8 |
| 225-250 | 6 | - | - | 6 |
| 250-275 | 7 | - | - | 7 |
| 275-300 | 2 | 2 | - | 4 |
| 300-350 | 6 | - | - | 6 |
| 350 & up | 4 | - | - | 4 |
| Totals | 457 | 85 | 57 | 599 |

The distribution of the combined survey figures is shown in Figure V, page 57.

The tax payments per occupant family, expressed as mean, median, and mode, are higher in the Lower Hill Survey than those from both the Terrace Village and Bedford Dwellings areas. The main reason

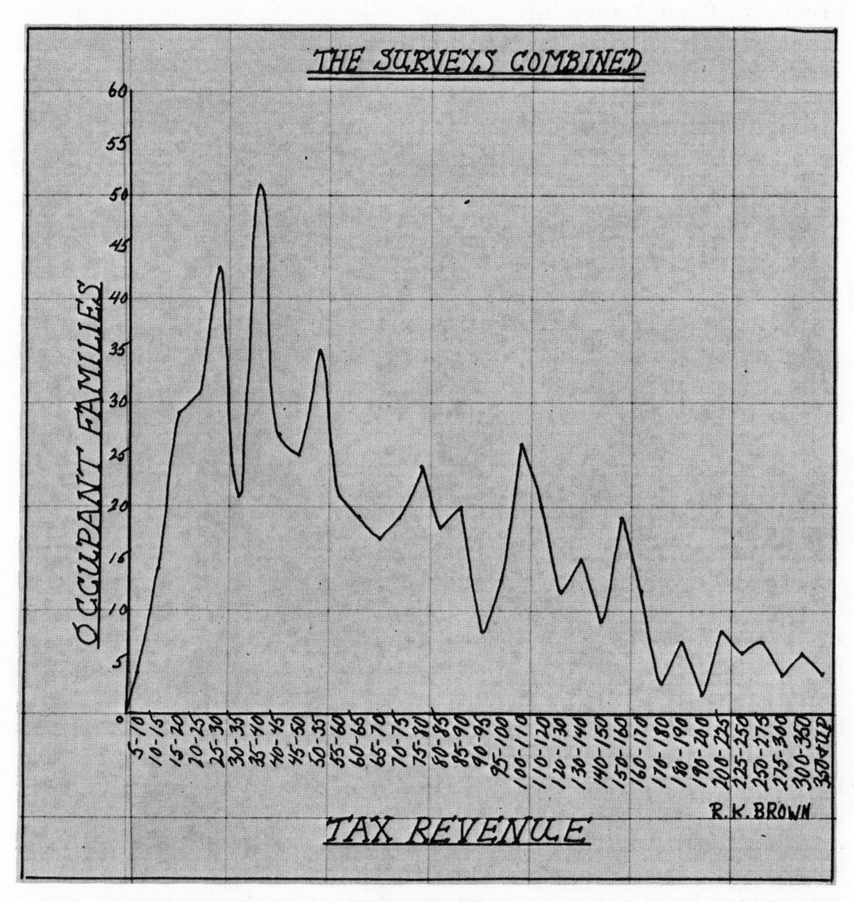


FIGURE V

for the difference is in the average land assessment per parcel in the three substandard areas. The average tax assessment on land per parcel in the three areas is as follows:

1. Lower Hill Survey . . . . . . . . . . . . . . . . . . $2,332.13
2. Terrace Village Survey . . . . . . . . . . . . . . 760.93
3. Bedford Dwellings Survey . . . . . . . . . . . . . 466.09

The average land assessment, therefore, is highest on Lower Hill land and then decreases per survey in much the same manner as the average tax payment from each survey area.

The writer believes that the higher land assessment in the Lower Hill area results from the fact that the geographic characteristics of a city play an important role in the determination of city land value.

Since Pittsburgh is restricted in size, available land is valued at a premium. Since Lower Hill is close to the downtown business district, its present residential value is enhanced by its potential commercial value. Lower Hill land, therefore, is assessed at a higher value than other areas further up on the Hill and at a distance from the business district. The average number of occupant families per dwelling in each survey area decreases correspondingly as follows:

1. Lower Hill Survey . . . . . . . . . . . . . . . . . . . . . . . . 2.5
2. Terrace Village Survey . . . . . . . . . . . . . . . . . . . . . 1.9
3. Bedford Dwellings Survey . . . . . . . . . . . . . . . . . . . 1.4

The data seem to indicate a trend relationship between the three substandard areas. This relationship is expressed in the average payment per occupant family, the average land assessment per parcel, and the average number of occupant families per dwelling unit.

## The Cost of Tax Exemption

As stated previously, the taxes paid on real property purchase for the taxpayer certain primary municipal services,[188] such as police protection, fire protection, public works, health and sanitation, public welfare and education. In theory, a portion of these taxes purchases for the local residents additional necessary services, such as municipal finance, administrative salaries, libraries, city planning functions, and maintenance of municipal lands and buildings.

In the final analysis, the local resident must pay all the municipal bills from refuse collection to the mayor's salary. The most equitable method of apportioning this financial burden would be to distribute it by tax among all those residents who use the municipal services and benefit from their operation. In theory, the local tax rate would be determined by dividing the municipal budget by the total of assessed valuations in the community.[189] The resulting percentile would be then applied to each property according to its taxable assessed valuation. On the basis of collection without any delinquencies, the budget amounts required for the purchase of municipal services would be obtained.

Unfortunately, the magnitude and complexities of modern municipal finance prohibit the attaining of such theoretical perfection. For illustrative purposes, however, let us assume that such is the method of obtaining municipal revenues and that property taxes furnish total municipal revenue. Further, assume that a community consists of ten properties of equal taxable value and that the cost of providing

188. The term "primary" is used to distinguish services which the taxpayer usually considers as purchased by his tax payment.

189. This theoretical statement does not include any consideration of other municipal tax income sources.

necessary municipal services, both primary and secondary, is one thousand dollars ($1,000.00).

Under such theoretical assumptions, each property owner would contribute one hundred dollars ($100.00); the necessary budgetary amount would be received by the local governing body, and the necessary municipal services would be made available to the ten taxpayers.

If, at some subsequent time, municipal authorities decide that two of the properties should be exempted from the paying of property taxes, an increased tax burden would be placed on the remaining eight taxpaying properties. Their respective tax burden would be increased from one hundred ($100.00) to one-hundred-twenty-five dollars ($125.00) each. Such a decision would have to be justified to the remaining eight taxpayers.

Fundamentally, this decision is justified because of the nature of the properties exempted from taxes, for they usually furnish some specific public, religious, or educational service. The taxpayers agree to the increased tax burden because of their desire to have such facilities available in the local community. Therefore, tax exemption is a contribution made by local taxpayers to the maintenance of these special-use properties.

The types of special-use properties exempted in Pittsburgh and the taxable valuation of the exempted properties is detailed in Table III, below.

The above example has over-simplified the process of tax exemption as it operates in actual practice, for the average resident does

TABLE III

Tax Exempt Property - City of Pittsburgh - 1954

| Property Type | Assessed Valuation | Per Cent of Total |
|---|---|---|
| City of Pittsburgh | $ 64,379,939.00 | 16.83 |
| Schools | 65,688,887.00 | 17.16 |
| Churches | 42,225,441.00 | 11.04 |
| Hospitals | 29,157,678.00 | 7.62 |
| Allegheny County | 14,836,095.00 | 3.88 |
| Other Utilities | 21,744,475.00 | 5.68 |
| Cemeteries | 6,561,080.00 | 1.72 |
| Railroads and Transportation | 65,697,102.00 | 17.17 |
| Commonwealth of Pennsylvania | 12,559,530.00 | 3.28 |
| Housing Authority | 27,799,326.00 | 7.26 |
| Non-Profit Organization | 9,889,805.00 | 2.58 |
| United States Government | 17,509,645.00 | 4.58 |
| Def. Projects | 4,574,320.00 | 1.20 |
| Total | $381,619,323.00 | 100.00 |

not participate directly in any decisions granting this privilage to certain properties. Many of the properties now enjoying tax exemption in Pittsburgh have been doing so for a period considerably longer than the life spans of many of the local residents now sharing the cost of providing services to the properties. In addition, property taxes do not contribute the total amount of funds required by the municipality for the purchase of such services.

Such tax exemptions are based on the fundamental premise that they are sound when applied to property with specific public, educational, or religious functions. The point to be emphasized is that the local taxpayer should be aware of his contributions through tax exemption to public-use properties. The writer believes that each tax exemption should be justified by some definite civic or social need. Tax exemption can be carried ad infinitum to the immediate detriment of tax-paying properties and ultimately to the detriment of the municipal tax base itself if some rational, economically feasible method is not established for determining what properties have the special-use characteristics that call for tax exemption.

The ultimate decision should be vested in the taxpayers who are going to share the additional burden created by the tax exemption privilege. The first step in reaching such a decision is to approximate the weight of the burden created by specific exemptions—in this instance, by Pittsburgh's public housing properties.

Previous data established that an average tax payment per occupant family in substandard areas contributed to Pittsburgh tax revenues; this payment has been compared to the average payment-in-lieu of taxes made on behalf of the low-income residents of the public housing projects. Both figures represent payments for municipal services furnished to these families. If the amount contributed per occupant family is compared with the city's cost for the municipal services furnished, the amount of subsidy made by other taxpayers towards the furnishing of services to these properties may be approximated.

*The Cost of Municipal Services.*

In the fiscal year ended December 31, 1955, the City of Pittsburgh experienced total expenditures in the amount of $49,374,702.33. Included in this total were expenditures of $43,124,151.20 from the General Fund and expenditures of $6,250,551.13 from the municipal Water Fund.[190]

The statistics reveal that the following amounts were expended for direct, or primary, services:

190. Annual Report of the City Comptroller for the Fiscal Period Ended December 31, 1955, City of Pittsburgh, Pennsylvania, p. 42.

| | |
|---|---|
| Public Health . . . . . . . . . . . . . | $ 3,010,652.29 |
| Public Safety . . . . . . . . . . . . . | 13,578,462.76 |
| Public Works . . . . . . . . . . . . . | 2,263,000.69 |
| City Refuse . . . . . . . . . . . . . | 3,599,016.96 |
| Parks and Recreation . . . . . . . | 2,536,677.82 |
| Highways and Sewers . . . . . . . | 2,585,689.57 |
| Total . . . . . . . . . . | $27,573,500.09 |

For other secondary services an additional expenditure of $21,801,202.24 came from the General Fund, and an expenditure of $6,250,551.13 came from the Water Fund.

The total amount of expenditures should be apportioned among the total number of dwelling units in order to ascertain the cost of furnishing services to each dwelling unit. Ultimately the occupants will pay all operating expenses, either through property or other taxes or through the debt service on past and/or future municipal borrowings.

The writer realizes that such an analysis is not as accurate as might be obtained by ascertaining and apportioning expenditures in the specific survey areas, but present municipal accounting techniques make no provision for population allocation of expenditures other than a per capita calculation. Although the bulk of municipal expenditures is allocated on a department basis, no further detailed allocation, such as by Ward or Census Tract, is available. This lack is due largely to the fact that many municipal departments supply service to portions of several wards or census tracts. Police precinct X, for example, will serve portions of Ward A and of Ward B.

Estimating an average expenditure per occupied dwelling unit on a city-wide basis should yield a mean cost below that which would result from similar analysis in the study's specific survey areas; as the size of the sample increases, variability among the sample means will decrease. In this instance, the whole statistical universe is being used rather than samples from it.

In addition, those in favor of public housing have stated that it costs the city more to furnish services to families in substandard areas than to families in decent, sanitary dwelling units.[191] The reduction of these costs is often given as one of the advantages accruing to a municipality by virtue of the existence of public housing units.

The United States Census of 1950 reported a total of 193,889 dwelling units in the City of Pittsburgh.[192] The total City of Pittsburgh expenditures of $49,374,702.33, apportioned among the total number of dwelling units, yields a mean cost per dwelling unit of $254.59, or

191. See What the Housing Act Can Do For Your City, United States Department of the Interior, United States Housing Authority, Washington, D.C., 1938, pp.36-40, for specific statistics relative to this advantage of public housing.

192. U.S. Bureau of the Census. U.S. Census of Housing: 1950. Vol. V, Block Statistics, Part 145 (Washington, 1952).

the cost to the City of Pittsburgh to furnish the various municipal services to each dwelling unit. Table IV illustrates the relationship between the cost of the services and the amount contributed per occupant family in the survey areas towards defraying this expense.

TABLE IV

Local Subsidy Amount per Occupant Family per Year

| Survey Area | Tax Payment per Occupant Family | Cost of Services | Amount of Differential |
|---|---|---|---|
| Lower Hill | $91.22 | $254.59 | $163.37 |
| Terrace Village | 56.67 | 254.59 | 197.92 |
| Bedford Dwellings | 45.21 | 254.59 | 209.38 |
| Public Housing | 39.09 | 254.59 | 215.50 |

*Municipal Income Sources.*

In the fiscal period ended December 31, 1955, the City of Pittsburgh received its income from the sources itemized in Table V.[193]

TABLE V

Income Sources—City of Pittsburgh—1955

| Income Source | Amount | Percent of Total |
|---|---|---|
| General Fund: | | |
| Real Property Taxes, Current Year | $23,108,592.00 | 48.42 |
| Real Property Taxes, Prior Years | 894,195.00 | 1.87 |
| Personal Property Taxes | 787,269.00 | 1.65 |
| Amusement Taxes | 1,039,577.00 | 2.18 |
| Mercantile Taxes | 2,555,270.00 | 5.36 |
| Earned Income Taxes | 6,013,872.00 | 12.60 |
| Penalties, Interest, Fines | 750,036.00 | 1.57 |
| Licenses and Permits | 1,259,604.00 | 2.64 |
| Rentals and Charges | 1,125,978.00 | 2.36 |
| Miscellaneous General Fund Income | 2,978,687.00 | 6.24 |
| Water Fund: | | |
| Metered Water | 6,097,631.00 | 13.01 |
| Flat Water Charge | 1,001,643.00 | 2.10 |
| Total | $47,723,508.00 | 100.00 |

193. Source: City of Pittsburgh, op. cit., p. 6.

Real property taxes contributed approximately 50 per cent of the total city revenue for the fiscal period January 1, 1955, to December 31, 1955.

The previous apportioning of the total municipal expenditures among the total number of dwelling units resulted in an average cost per dwelling unit of $254.59. One might argue that since real property taxes did not contribute the total amount of municipal income, apportioning the total amount of expenditures will include income from other sources.

If this claim is assumed as valid, the apportionment analysis can be predicated on the following theory: Since real property taxes contributed approximately 50 percent of the total municipal revenue during the fiscal period, the same percentage of the cost of municipal services was purchased by the payment of these taxes.[194] Therefore, an estimate of the actual subsidy amount should be based on the difference between the amount paid by real property taxes rather than on the basis of total municipal expenditures. In this instance, the average cost per dwelling unit of $254.59 would be divided by the 50 percentile; $127.30 would be the amount of the average cost of municipal services paid by real property taxes.

When this figure is substituted for the average based on total municipal expenditures, the analysis still reveals a difference between the amount contributed by tax towards the payment for municipal services and the cost of the services. With specific reference to the survey areas, the differential exists in the following amounts:

TABLE VI

Local Subsidy Amount per Occupant Family per Year

| Survey Area | Tax Payment per Occupant Family | Cost of Services | Amount of Differential |
|---|---|---|---|
| Lower Hill | $91.22 | $127.30 | $36.08 |
| Terrace Village | 56.67 | 127.30 | 70.63 |
| Bedford Dwellings | 45.21 | 127.30 | 82.09 |
| Public Housing | 39.09 | 127.30 | 88.21 |

These findings indicate that a subsidy does exist as a result of the differential between tax payment and service cost. Further, this amount is paid by some source other than the families receiving the

194. Fifty per cent of the City of Pittsburgh's expenditures during the fiscal period January 1, 1955, to December 31, 1955, equals $24,374,702.33. Total real estate tax income; both for current and past years, for the same fiscal period equals $24,002,787.00.

services; presumably this amount is contributed by other taxpaying property in the City of Pittsburgh.

The results of this analysis indicate the following reasonable conclusion: public housing is not bearing its fair share of the cost of municipal services furnished to the project tenants. The fact that the slum areas are not paying their fair share either is an accepted fact and one of the cardinal reasons for eliminating slum areas from the city. Therefore, that which replaces the slum dwelling should alleviate this condition. Yet the study results indicate that public housing projects require a larger subsidy than the slum housing area.

Raising the percentage of shelter rents paid in lieu of taxes might be an obvious answer. This, however, would be only a partial solution to the problem, for it is concerned with only one part of the subsidy contribution made to the projects. The solution must be further reaching if adequate results are to be realized.

Part Three

# CONCLUSIONS AND RECOMMENDATIONS

CHAPTER SIX

# The Problems

Two major housing problems confront the urban community. First is the problem of insuring as best it can the maintenance of a healthful and sanitary living environment for its citizens. The community must use every means at its disposal to secure a minimum standard of housing for all its families. Variations above this minimum will depend upon the initiative of the individual family unit. If the means do not exist in a community for pursuing this goal, the community must then create some constitutional means to fill the void.

Second, the community must create a high quality level of real property by the construction of new buildings; the upgrading of existing dilapidated, but salvable, houses; and the demolition of those which are beyond repair. Then the community must maintain the quality of its physical inventory at as high a level as possible.

The over-all problem is a composite one. The quality of residential dwellings must be upgraded, by the means subsequently described, before the community can hope to approach the attainment of a sanitary living environment for a substantial portion of its population. If progress is made in the quality improvement of residential structures, the creation of a healthful living environment should follow as a matter of course. Maintaining structural and environmental components becomes the important consideration.

The extinction of the slum will require complete citizen support of a well-planned and executed program comprising both the eradication of existing slum areas and the institution of measures to forestall the regrowth of future slum areas. Relatively speaking, slum eradication will include the short-term aspects of the program; slum protection will encompass the facets of a long-range point of view. Instituted together and operating concurrently, the two approaches will enable the citizens of a community to rid their urban neighborhoods of existing slums and eliminate their reoccurrence. The elimination of existing slum areas, without any provision for prevention of future slums, would be a futile gesture, though it is the more important from the point of immediacy. An effective slum-clearance program must provide for both slum elimination and slum prevention.

The eradication of substandard housing areas can be accomplished by the employment of two devices. The first involves the enactment and enforcement of local housing codes which specify certain minimum standards of construction and sanitation. This approach would be directed towards those dwellings whose repair would not exceed the costs of replacing them with new structures. Where the structure is considered to be beyond repair, the second device would be used: the dwelling would be demolished. If a structure must be destroyed, however, its demolition should be undertaken as a corollary function of neighborhood preservation. Demolition should be utilized only as a last alternative, never as a substitute for repair and modernization.

CHAPTER SEVEN

# The Local Housing Code

Many of the urban communities which are confronted with the prospect of slum eradication have had various housing and sanitation codes on their statutes for many years.[195] But the physical inventory of these communities continued to decline, primarily because their codes had not been enforced.[196]

Slum eradication demands one of two things in regard to local housing and sanitation codes. Those in existence must be modernized to include both a comprehensive list of minimum standards and the means of enforcing conformity to these standards. If the codes are so outdated as to be beyond modernization, they should be replaced with new codes which, again, provide enforceable minimum standards. The present trend in American urban communities is towards the second alternative.[197]

The enforcement of a housing code is not an easy task, nor is the investigation incident to enforcement a simple accomplishment. Both require the active support of all citizens: the landlords who do not

195. Roy Wenzlick, "As I See It," The Real Estate Analyst, (St. Louis, July 22, 1949), p. 288.

196. In many instances the codes could not be enforced effectively because no means was provided for the prosecution of violators. This factor was coupled in some cases with the dilatory attitude of local enforcement agencies.

197. A survey published by the Housing and Home Finance Agency in 1956 contained an analysis of the housing codes of 56 representative American cities. The total number of cities, ranging in population size from 6,906 to 2,071,605 and having an average population of 306,270, had begun to enact effective housing codes only since 1948. The greater percentage of the codes had been enacted in the period 1953-1955. Housing and Home Finance Agency, Provisions of Housing Codes in Various American Cities, Urban Renewal Bulletin Number 3 (Washington, 1956), pp. 1-2.

want to improve their properties; the tenants who do not want their quarters improved at the cost of an increase in rent; the politicians who will frame the code requirements and seek their enforcement; the many other citizens whose passive attitude towards the quality of housing in their community helped to foster the spread of slums. Effective housing code enforcement seems to promise great returns for this cooperation.

The benefits to be derived from the initiation and effective enforcement of a properly constructed housing code are reflected in statistics by the Public Health Service relative to its study in Baltimore, Maryland, of the changes which occurred in the quality of housing after the enforcement of a housing code.[198] Comparison of the "before" and "after" data revealed the following results:

(a) The average dwelling score of deficiency decreased by 35.5 per cent.

(b) The average sub-total score of deficiency for facilities decreased by 13.4 per cent.

(c) The average sub-total score of deficiency for maintenance decreased 74.2 per cent.

(d) The average sub-total for occupancy decreased 7.2 per cent.

(e) The percentage of owner-occupancy remained constant at 41.5 per cent.

(f) The average shelter rent increased $6.40, from $36.40 to $42.80, per dwelling unit per month.

(g) The median family income increased from $239.00 per month to $259.00 per month.

The survey disclosed

> . . . that the enforcement effort resulted in significant improvement of the quality of housing in the pilot area without untoward effect on the residents. As a matter of fact, the improved dwellings are more healthful and safer places in which to live. Furthermore, the improvement in maintenance scores alone should insure that the useful life of these dwellings will be significantly extended.[199]

The only alternative to the upgrading of housing through the effective enforcement of a local housing code seems to be the gradual disintegration of the community itself. The impact of the slum is being experienced today by an ever-widening circle of citizens, many of whom found it once difficult to comprehend the viciousness and rapidity with which slum blight attacks and destroys physically and economically sound structures. Fortunately, this awakening of civic responsibility is beginning to reach significant proportions. It offers

198. Public Health Service, U.S. Department of Health, Education and Welfare, Housing Rehabilitation and Enforcement of Housing Laws (Washington, 1955), p. 34.

199. Ibid.

the greatest hope of urban salvation through the necessary community effort.

## The Problem of Community Education

Coupled with the institution of an effectively enforced housing code and the utilization, where necessary, of the process of urban demolition and renewal is the need for community education. Slums have resulted primarily from the activity or inactivity of people: landlords who have neglected to make necessary repairs to properties, tenants who have not attempted to bear a reasonable portion of the burden of property maintenance, and other citizens whose passive attitude contributed indirectly to the spread of slum blight.

A comprehensive housing program should provide for the education of landlords and future renters as to their respective responsibility for property maintenance. Education should include instruction on accepted maintenance techniques. Above all, the program should inculcate all residents with a knowledge of the benefits to be gained through conformity with established minimum housing standards.

The formation of civic improvement associations should be encouraged in every neighborhood to serve as the nucleus for a permanent community effort of housing maintenance, for the program of housing rejuvenation being proposed is a community affair. Each neighborhood must build up an alert population, "who will be able to see the advantages in having a 'renewed' environment, and who will have the know-how to keep it that way."[200] The success or failure of an enforcement program will depend directly on the cooperative action of all residents, since they stand to gain or lose in direct proportion to the advances made against slum blight. Support should be enlisted by the dissemination of pertinent information through the above neighborhood groups and through the other media of communication.

A program of education is an essential ingredient of a housing program, for it will help to promote the essential community action. "Before a neighborhood will be truly renewed, the experts recognize, the people living in it will have to learn how to cope with the ever-present pressures that would exploit it again."[201]

## The Problem of Code Rigidity

The requirements of housing codes must be attuned to the prevailing construction practices and techniques in each specific locality. The great danger inherent in the creation and attempted enforcement of

200. Martin Millspaugh, What Is Urban Renewal? New Face for American Committee of the National Association of Home Builders, National Housing Center (Washington, 1956), p. 14.
201. Ibid.

rigid standards must be avoided by careful examination of each standard in a community's housing code. Prevailing techniques and code standards must co-exist, since the enforcement of minimum requirements seems to imply the upgrading of substandard units to at least the minimum level prevailing in the community.

The following list of general standards, developed by the Build America Better Council of the National Association of Real Estate Boards, indicates some of the more fundamental aspects which should be provided for in the enactment and enforcement of housing codes:[202]

(1) Inside running water, flush toilet, and bathing facilities with sewer connections and proper ventilation in each dwelling unit.

(2) Adequate heating equipment.

(3) A properly maintained dwelling, in good repair, and kept structurally safe and weatherproof.

(4) Plumbing maintained in sanitary and workable condition.

(5) Adequate light, air, and ventilation.

(6) Specifications for occupied basement rooms, if they are permitted.

(7) Specifications for the maximum number of persons allowed per room (usually not more than an average of 1-1/2).

(8) All dwellings, yards, and open spaces kept clean and free from accumulations of dirt, vermin, and debris.

(9) Definite responsibility placed upon the occupier of the premises for exterior sanitary and other conditions.

(10) Specifications for size, cubage, and ventilation of sleeping rooms.

(11) Provisions that the proper municipal official or department, after due notice to the occupant or owner, or both, may correct any violation of the health, fire, sanitary or other related code and charge the property with a lien, or that he have power, when necessary, to order the property vacated.

(12) Stiff fines for each day of continued violation imposed against the owner, occupant, or both.

## The Problem of Finance

One of the objections to the practicability of effective housing and sanitation code enforcement has been the claimed or actual lack of a source of funds necessary to effect property improvements. It is one thing, the critics claim, to tell an owner to rehabilitate his property, but it is quite another thing to secure enforcement of the order when he does not have the financial resources to effect the repairs. Further,

202. Build America Better Council, National Association of Real Estate Boards, Blueprint for Neighborhood Conservation, (Henry J. Kaiser Company, 1956), p. 12.

no accepted source of finance provides for a loan of such funds to the property owner. The owner is thus faced with a paradoxical problem. Even if he has the desire to make his property comply with the housing code, he is forced, out of economic necessity, to refuse. If the code is being effectively enforced, the owner's failure to comply results in a fine, the affixing of a municipal lien on the property if the municipality undertakes the repairs, and ultimate foreclosure and sale of the property. Through no apparent fault of his own, the distraught property owner is deprived of the title to his property.

The incidence of this disadvantage falls primarily upon many property owners in the older, "close-in" urban residential neighborhoods. It affects particularly older potential borrowers with low incomes or pensions whose real purchasing power is being reduced through inflation. By definition, other factors remaining equal, a younger person is a better mortgage risk if for no other reason than that he is expected to live beyond the term of the loan. This situation, coupled with the older person's reduced real income, causes him serious difficulty.

Some method of finance must be provided so that the owners of properties not meeting the minimum requirements of the housing code can secure the financial means for making necessary repairs and improvements. If the program of housing code enforcement is to function properly and make its vital contribution to the preservation of urban communities, it must be administered in a constructive fashion. The absence of a satisfactory source of loan funds, available to all owners whose properties qualify structurally, militates against public acceptance and support of enforcement of a housing code. Not only will effective endorsement be curtailed, but also the application of any enforcement procedures will be achieved in a negative, punitive fashion.

The precepts of a private enterprise system indicate that the impetus behind a lending program should come from the fraternity of private lending agencies. They stand to benefit greatly from the effects of housing code endorsement. Not only will they be receiving sound physical collateral as security for improvement loans made, but the over-all upgrading of the urban housing inventory should increase the value of other residential investments they might have.

The Federal Government, recognizing belatedly the necessity for a source of available improvement and modernization loan funds, has sought to encourage private lenders to make such loans, by offering as an inducement the benefits of the Federal Housing Administration insurance program. Accordingly, incorporated in the United States Housing Act of 1954[203] was a new Section 220 program which authorized Federal Housing Administration mortgage insurance for the rehabilitation of existing dwellings in slum clearance and urban

203. Public Law 560, 83rd Congress, August 2, 1954.

redevelopment areas where Federal aid was being extended under Title I of the United States Housing Act of 1949.[204] In addition, the Housing Act of 1954 contained a new Section 221 program which provides Federal Housing Administration mortgage insurance for low-cost housing for displaced persons in a community where slum clearance and urban renewal and redevelopment programs, under Title I of the Housing Act of 1949, were programmed.[205]

These two programs, although designed to aid lower-income families, do not offer much assistance for those families in the lowest income levels or those families whose incomes lie somewhere between the lower availability limits of these programs and the upper limits of the lowest income group. This situation was made apparent by the inclusion in both the Housing Acts of 1954 and 1956 of authorizations for additional public housing units. After twenty-five years of operation of the public housing program, the problems still exist.

A stratum of low-income families seems inevitably to require public housing rental aid. If a community is to administer effectively a comprehensive housing program, it must provide for assistance to its needy, low-income families who may be forced to vacate substandard housing. Since, in all likelihood, the seriousness of this situation will not decrease substantially in the foreseeable future, the problem is still to provide some equitable means for furnishing housing aid so as to reach as significant a portion of the low-income group as possible.

---

204. Mortgage limits were the same on 1- to 4-family dwellings as under the regular Section 203 sales housing program, except that structures with more than 4-family dwelling units could be covered; in such cases, the mortgage limits were $35,000.00 plus, not to exceed $7,000.00 for each family unit in excess of four. See Housing and Home Finance Agency, Office of the Administrator, Brief Summary of the Housing Act of 1954 (Washington, 1954), p. 3.

205. The maximum mortgage amount available under this Section was established at $7,600.00 or $8,600.00 in high-cost areas and 95 per cent of value. Owner-occupants utilizing this program are required to make an equity down-payment of at least five per cent. The maturity of Section 221 mortgages is not to exceed thirty years or three-fourths of the remaining economic life of the property, whichever is lower. The interest rate is five per cent, but it can be increased to six per cent if necessary to meet the demands of the mortgage market. Ibid., pp. 3-4.

CHAPTER EIGHT

# The Paradox of Public Housing

The public housing program, as presently constituted, is not capable of furnishing the required aid on a scale which will begin to approach the dimensions of the problem.

The prevailing theory on subsidized housing results in the maintenance of a low-rent level by means of direct Government subsidies and a circumvention of usual tax assessment procedures. The tax exemption provisions, in turn, result in a reduced tax income for the city because the in-lieu payments are lower than actual tax payments.

Today public housing takes care of only a small part of the low-income group. A substantial majority of the low-income group must pay either taxes on its own property or indirect taxes in the form of rent payments to landlords who, in turn, pay full taxes on assessed valuations. Available statistics indicate that more than 95 per cent of the low-income group in the City of Pittsburgh who could qualify for public housing are paying full taxes on assessed valuations directly or through rental payments. The 1950 United States Census of Population shows that out of a total sample of 231,325 families and unrelated individuals in the City of Pittsburgh, 155,515 had incomes of $3,499.00 or less.[206] When this figure is placed beside the available number of the City's public housing units, i.e., 7,011 units, the percentage above is realized. If this number of low-income families is multiplied by an average cost per new public housing unit of $10,000.00 (a low approximation), the initial cost of construction alone is seen to be prohibitive.

As a result of this situation, the majority of the low-income group

206. U.S. Census of Population, U.S. Department of Commerce, Bulletin P-D43 (Washington, 1943), Vol. III, Chapter 43, p. 8. 231,325 is broken down into approximately 180,000 families and 50,000 unrelated individuals.

is helping to support the minority of its group living in the City's public housing projects. Charles B. Shattuck, in 1953, placed the cost of each public housing unit constructed since 1946 at approximately $11,600.00 per unit. Assume that a family purchases a home costing the same amount, i.e., $11,600.00. Assume further that the home is financed under the existing Federal Housing Administration or Veterans Administration requirements. This family agrees voluntarily to make amortized payments of interest and principal on the mortgage debt and to pay taxes on the assessed valuation of the property. A portion of this tax payment is used to pay for a portion of the services furnished the non-taxpaying occupants of public housing units. Thus, this home-owning family must help support, theoretically, another family of equal size and income in a public housing unit; the inequity of the situation becomes evident.

Government financial participation in the public housing program has necessitated the investment of a large sum of money. The subsidy concept which is the very basis of the program depends for its fulfillment on the gift or grant of funds by government, Federal and local, to the local housing authorities. The benefits achieved through subsidy are passed along to the tenant by virtue of the low rental he pays.

The resident taxpayers of a community contribute to the subsidy by paying the difference between the local authority's in-lieu payments and taxes otherwise obtainable. The taxpayers at large pay the Federal grant. This study has indicated that public housing draws a substantial subsidy through tax exemption at the local government level. Apparently a majority of the low-income group subsidizes a minority of its own group in public housing projects because of this local contribution.

The main social justification for the initiation and continuation of the Federal public housing program has been based on the premise of need. Fundamentally, public effort programs, such as that of public housing, must be justified by the existence of a definite need for the programs.

At the time the housing program was established, housing for low-income families was seriously short, whereas substandard dwellings—presumably occupied in the main by this same low-income group—were in excess. This situation enforced the belief that private enterprise was not making any substantial efforts toward meeting the need of the low-income group for decent, sanitary housing at a price the low-income family could afford.

Subsequently and, in part, consequently, the Federal public housing program was launched with the alleviation of the low-income group's housing shortage as one of its objectives.[207] Subsequent expansion of

207. Other effects were hoped for when the program was first initiated under the auspices of the Housing Division of the Public Works Administration. For a detailed analysis of these anticipated effects, see pages 5 and 6.

the program's scope has been based on this same fundamental premise of need.

Few can argue with the basic contention of advocates of public housing—that the low-income family needs assistance in its quest for decent housing. Notwithstanding that public housing has made no appreciable addition to the pool of housing available for the low-income public group, public housers believe that, because of the need, the number of physical units added has been far better than none at all.

The continuation of any particular public program, such as public housing, that entails the expenditure of public monies, must be considered on the basis of an existing need. Once the need is established, the contemplated program must be then analyzed in terms of its capacity to meet this need, either partially or, preferably, completely. This analysis should apply both to proposed programs and to those already in existence.

An outworn or inadequate system should not be kept in existence simply because a perfect substitute cannot be made immediately. Improvement must be attempted even if it means only one step toward perfection. Obviously, an existing program's prior operating experience should weigh heavily in any evaluation of its merits.

Previous statistics have indicated that the public housing program has not made any substantial inroads into the problem of supplying a ". . . decent home and a suitable living environment for every American family"[208]—this, despite the addition of 489,744 units of public housing space.[209] The program, to date, has apparently failed to achieve even a temporary solution to the housing problems of the majority of the low-income group, let alone a lasting solution.

The fact that the public housing program has failed to effect a solution to the problem should not be interpreted as a direct indictment of the program and its various coordinating officials, both national and local. The writer believes that those connected with the administration of the public housing program have made a conscientious effort toward fulfilling the program's stated objectives.

The basic fault lies within the framework of the program as it is presently constituted, for it must fight against two formidable opponents: time and dollars. In addition, all new housing is faced with a struggle against depreciation. In actual application, the officials' fight is revealed in several ways.

First, a great deal of time is required to add new units of residential space in any appreciable quantity, whether public or privately owned housing. Second, a great deal of money is needed to add the new units. Third, with the factors of time and money militating against the rapid addition of new units, depreciation is operating to reduce

208. Declaration of National Housing Policy, Section 2, The Housing Act of 1949, Public Law 171, 81st Congress, July 15, 1949.

209. Housing and Home Finance Agency, 9th Annual Report, Part III, (Washington, 1955), p. 325.

constantly the quality level of existing dwelling units: the "filtering-down" process is in operation.

In essence, the public housing program, as presently constituted, is not equipped to function at a level which will enable it to achieve its objectives. The need for some public policy program which will be able to make substantial progress in providing a decent home for every American family is just as real today as it was in 1933 or 1937.

In the City of Pittsburgh, the failure of the public housing program to upgrade appreciably the quality of the total supply of housing for the low-income group has been compounded by the existence of a paradoxical situation.

The quality of housing in Pittsburgh is far below the ideal of a decent home for every resident family, especially so among the low-income group. Since the number of public housing units comprises only a small percentage of the total number of dwelling units in the City of Pittsburgh, one might expect a huge demand for these units because the existence of a large number of low-income families and a small number of sanitary, low-rent units available to them. Certainly the desires of the Housing Authority of the City of Pittsburgh to construct additional units of public housing, plans for which are well underway, lend credence to such an assumption.[210] The facts, however, prove otherwise, for the Authority has experienced a general upward trend in vacancies in the period July 1, 1955 to December 26, 1956. See Table VII, page 79. Despite the increasing number of vacancies, the number of applications the Authority has received, as detailed in Table VIII, page 80, has been fairly stable.

As indicated in Table VII, vacancies existed in all of the various projects, ranging as of December 26, 1956, from 21.4 per cent in Glen-Hazel Heights project to 0.8 per cent in Broadhead Manor project. The vacancy percentages increased appreciably from July 1, 1955 to July 2, 1956 and then decreased slightly by December 26, 1956. Notable examples of this general upward trend have been projects Allegheny Dwellings, St. Clair Village, Glen-Hazel Heights, and Arlington Heights. Several reasons for the increased vacancies in these projects follow:

(1) Glen-Hazel Heights, operated until February, 1953 as a Lanham Act project, was a War Housing Leased project. The rental schedule of the project was established at higher rental rates than the truly low-rent projects owned and operated by the Authority. In February, 1953, ownership of the project was conveyed to the City of Pittsburgh, which was obligated to convert it into a low-rent project. Consequently, at the time of ownership transfer, Glen-Hazel Heights had a substantial percentage of families whose incomes exceeded the

210. Currently the Authority has begun to acquire the site for a 999-unit project to be located in the North Side area of the city. In addition, two other projects have received preliminary Federal approval.

TABLE VII

Vacancy Trends—Public Housing Projects—City of Pittsburgh[211]

| Project | 7/1/55 No. of Units | 7/1/55 Per Cent Vacant | 1/3/56 No. of Units | 1/3/56 Per Cent Vacant | 7/2/56 No. of Units | 7/2/56 Per Cent Vacant | 12/26/56 No. of Units | 12/26/56 Per Cent Vacant |
|---|---|---|---|---|---|---|---|---|
| PA-1-1 | 66 | 8.2 | 97 | 12.1 | 116 | 14.5 | 53 | 6.6 |
| PA-1-2,8 | - | -- | - | - | 19 | 2.2 | 3 | .4 |
| PA-1-3 | 28 | 1.5 | 29 | 1.6 | 53 | 2.9 | 41 | 2.2 |
| PA-1-4 | 67 | 10.2 | 92 | 13.9 | 102 | 15.5 | 81 | 12.3 |
| PA-1-5 | 2 | .7 | 4 | 1.4 | 3 | 1.1 | 12 | 4.2 |
| PA-1-6 | 3 | .7 | 3 | .7 | 3 | .7 | 7 | .8 |
| PA-1-7 | - | -- | 48 | 4.4 | 40 | 3.7 | 90 | 8.2 |
| PA-1-10 | 12 | 1.2 | 68 | 6.8 | 61 | 6.1 | 96 | 21.4 |
| Totals | 178 | 2.5% | 341 | 4.9% | 397 | 5.7% | 383 | 5.4% |

low-income requirements of the public housing program. The Authority was faced with the task of clearing the projects of these families and incurring substantial vacancies until the space could be re-occupied by families meeting the eligibility requirements. The units should have been occupied as soon as the over-income families moved out, but they were not. The Authority has met with prospective tenant resistance primarily because of the general run-down condition, a situation fostered by the peculiarities of the project's war-time status.[212] Glen-Hazel Heights is not an appealing home even for many low-income families.[213]

(2) St. Clair Village is the most recently completed of the Authority's public housing projects. The Authority has attempted, from its inception, to integrate white and negro families in this project. This plan has engendered white tenant resistance. In the words of one Authority official, "Everytime a negro family goes to the project, even for a look-see, there are three or four white families that come in the next day and give notice that they want to cancel their leases." This tremendous resistance to integration has contributed substantially to the number of vacancies in the project.

211. Figures were compiled from the Daily Reports of the project managers as of the dates indicated. Total percentages were computed on the basis of 7,011 units of public housing.

212. See pages 40 and 76-77.

213. Two types of families are within the general category, "low-income family." The first type is that which is almost destitute and will accept housing no matter where it is. The second type has enough economic means to justify its right to a choice of home. This second type of low-income family has resisted moving into Glen-Hazel Heights.

## TABLE VIII

Housing Authority of the City of Pittsburgh
Applications Received and Referred
Tenant Selection Division

| YEAR | APPLICATIONS | | | | | | | | | | |
|---|---|---|---|---|---|---|---|---|---|---|---|
| | Received | | | Requested | | | Referred | | | Rejected | |
| | Total | White | Negro | Total | White | Negro | Total | White | Negro | White | Negro |
| 1949 | 2483 | 1457 | 1026 | 1011 | 748 | 263 | 998 | 740 | 258 | - | - |
| 1950 | 2386 | 1325 | 1061 | 991 | 743 | 248 | 911 | 707 | 204 | - | - |
| 1951 | 2483 | 1350 | 1133 | 1053 | 808 | 245 | 1012 | 720 | 292 | 67 | 16 |
| 1952 | 2516 | 1360 | 1156 | 1064 | 852 | 212 | 1131 | 924 | 207 | 292 | 42 |
| 1953 | 3166 | 1883 | 1283 | 1778 | 1345 | 433 | 1662 | 1233 | 429 | 339 | 58 |
| 1954 | 4056 | 2457 | 1559 | 2539 | 1776 | 763 | 2472 | 1719 | 751 | 440 | 137 |
| 1955 | 3069 | 1901 | 1168 | 2129 | 1688 | 441 | 1771 | 1376 | 395 | 355 | 70 |
| 1956 | | | | | | | | | | | |
| Jan. | 240 | 146 | 94 | 144 | 117 | 27 | 131 | 108 | 23 | 11 | 3 |
| Feb. | 275 | 159 | 116 | 74 | 59 | 15 | 130 | 109 | 21 | 18 | 3 |
| Mar. | 244 | 145 | 99 | 130 | 122 | 17 | 95 | 85 | 10 | 26 | 8 |
| April | 226 | 156 | 70 | 93 | 70 | 23 | 113 | 95 | 18 | 27 | 4 |
| May | 237 | 166 | 71 | 163 | 122 | 41 | 121 | 109 | 12 | 24 | - |
| June | 143 | 91 | 44 | 79 | 52 | 27 | 75 | 68 | 7 | 19 | 1 |

(3) Arlington Heights project is located on the South Side of the city. Most of the residents surrounding the project are employed by the neighboring steel mills, characteristically, their incomes have been higher than the public housing limits. Since these families do not qualify for rentals in the Arlington Heights project, low-income tenants for this project must be relocated from other areas. Resistance from prospective tenants has resulted, for the low-income family, as a rule, desires to locate in familiar surroundings.[214] The proximity of Arlington Heights to St. Clair Village is an important factor, also. A prospective tenant, upon looking at Arlington Heights and then looking across the valley at St. Clair Village, immediately prefers the newer project.

(4) Allegheny Dwellings project is experiencing difficulties because of integration efforts. Again, the result has been increasing tenant resistance and an upward trend in its vacancy rate.

Officials of the Authority are hard pressed to justify the existence of vacancies in the projects, especially in view of their desire to implement the Authority's present portfolio of housing units by the addition of still more units. The decision to initiate and continue policies of integration is questionable. The consequences of attempted integration might be more serious than the existence of vacant units, for a policy of "open-tenancy" would tend to isolate each project area more so than the income limitations have already done; the projects could become economic and social ghettos.

The fundamental point seems to be the problem of existing need and the ability of the program to satisfy this need. If a negro family is in need of public housing and qualifies for it, should it be denied admittance? Should the unit remain vacant until a white family decides to occupy it?

Previous data have established the existence of a definite need for sanitary, low-rent housing in Pittsburgh; the limits of this need extend far and above the capacity of existing public housing units. Yet, paradoxically, 5.8 per cent of the total number of public housing units in the City of Pittsburgh are vacant, and the number of applications received is stable. The situation becomes more complex because of the presence in the projects of families whose incomes are above the maximum permissible income limits of the Authority. Table IX, page 82, indicates that, as of December 31, 1955, 5.2 per cent of all project tenants were over the permissible income limits.

The Authority's desire to build more units seems inconsistent with the existing vacancy situation and the presence of over-income families in project units; vacancies usually indicate an over-supply of

214. This factor was revealed vividly by the Lower Hill Population Survey conducted by the Pittsburgh Housing Association. The overwhelming preference of the families being relocated in other areas was the Upper Hill, just beyond the demolition area.

TABLE IX

Over-Income Families in Public Housing Projects[215]
City of Pittsburgh

| Project Name | Percentage of Over-Income Tenants |
|---|---|
| Addison Terrace | 3.5% |
| Bedford Dwellings )<br>Bedford Dwellings Addition) | 2.4 |
| Wadsworth )<br>Allequippa Terrace ) | 3.9 |
| Arlington Heights | 4.2 |
| Allegheny Dwellings | 1.5 |
| Broadhead Manor | 2.9 |
| St. Clair Village | .8 |
| Glen-Hazel Heights | 18.9 |

competing space. A program which contemplates the aggravation of an existing adverse situation cannot contain much hope of a permanent solution to a problem as important and as broad in scope as that of eventually providing ". . . a decent home and a suitable living environment for every American family."

As previously illustrated, the subject of public housing has been and remains an extremely volatile issue. The attitudes of public housers, private real estate groups, and other interested parties, however, are undergoing change. Opposition to the existing public housing system seems to have resulted from its prior sporadic, often undefined, state. Discussions concerning the existing system of low-rent housing subsidy and its capabilities, both present and potential, are becoming more rational and realistic. As a result, opposition to the program has been based more on objective analysis than on subjective emotional reasoning and thus has become solidified. Granted, opposing views still exist, but the barriers to intelligent discussion have been lowered by the recognition of the enormity of the housing problems confronting the nation. Accurately described by many experts as the nation's number one domestic issue, the housing problem is at last receiving the concentrated and cooperative attention that it has needed for so long.

In effect, the long-range planning required in urban preservation and renewal has necessitated the examination of every facet of national and municipal housing policy, since the over-all revitalization of urban areas demands the institution and sustained pursuance of an integrated housing program. Certainly one of the chief components of

215. Percentages have been compiled from reports made to the Administrator of the Authority at the time of the Annual Report for 1955.

such an approach would seem to be the institution of a public policy program to aid needy, low-income families residing in slum areas. The apparent necessity for this aid, coupled with the need for a successful, financially feasible approach, has raised serious doubt in the minds of both public housing opponents and proponents as to the program's ability to provide an adequate amount of low-rent housing within the framework of existing socio-economic conditions.

The emergence of this questioning attitude is especially significant, since some of the suggestions for change have come from persons closely allied with the public housing program. Catherine Bauer, former director of research and information for the United States Housing Authority and a recognized authority on the subject of low-rent housing, has analyzed the existing situation as follows:

> Public housing has not followed the normal pattern for reform movements in modern democratic countries. Every social experiment starts off as an abstract idea . . . after it has been tried out for a while, one of two things usually happens. Either it dies off, an acknowledged failure, or it 'takes' and is accepted as an integral part of the ordinary scheme of things. . . . But public housing, after more than two decades, still drags along in a kind of limbo, continuously controversial, not dead but never more than half alive. . . . If the dreary deadlock is to be broken, it is first necessary to figure what really ails the program.[216]

Miss Bauer's desire to discover and correct possible program deficiencies is representative of the recent swell of informed opinion emanating from many housing experts. Opinion seems unanimous that a new, more realistic approach to the low-rent housing problem is necessary. The open expression of widespread concern and the actual attempt to solve the existing urban housing problems promise some progress. Already various alternative proposals have been suggested as housing experts in all fields attempt to find a workable solution to the apparent paradox of public housing.

Architectural Forum magazine presented in June, 1957, a compendium of the opinions of eleven housing experts on the subject of how to break the "dreary deadlock" of public housing.[217] Despite the variances in their professional backgrounds and the resultant differences of viewpoint, these experts were "remarkably consistent in their conclusions . . . that need for drastic action is already clear."[218] Though general in content, the concern expressed and the alternative

216. Catherine Bauer, "The Dreary Deadlock of Public Housing," Architectural Forum, May, 1957, p. 140.
217. The eleven experts are: James W. Rouse, Ellen Lurie, William L. C. Wheaton, Charles Abrams, Henry Churchill, Stanley Tankel, Dorothy Montgomery, Elizabeth Wood, Vernon Demars, Lee F. Johnson, and Carl Feiss.
218. "The Dreary Deadlock of Public Housing and How to Break It," Architectural Forum, June, 1957, p. 139.

solutions offered resulted in fairly well-defined conclusions. Briefly, they are as follows:[219]

(a) In order to overcome one of the apparent deficiencies of the present manner of subsidy, it was suggested that project tenants should not be evicted if their incomes rise above the maximum allowable limits. Rather, they should be encouraged to stay either by allowing the purchase of their unit on a cooperative basis or by the payment of an economic rental.

(b) The suggestion was made that the availability of units meeting minimum health and structural standards should be broadened considerably by opening the subsidy plan to private builders and allowing all types of dwellings, new or old, to participate.

(c) A change in the basic form of subsidy was recommended; in effect, the subsidy would be shifted from housing projects to individual families.

(d) In order to achieve a much greater diffusion of low-income families throughout a community rather than a solidification of them in project areas, discontinuing the erection of projects altogether was recommended.

(e) Since much of the criticism of the existing program seems to stem from its lack of adaptability and flexibility, determining the manner of subsidy on a purely local level was suggested to replace set Federal Government procedures. In addition, the suggestion was made that the system of local authorities, required by the existing legislation, be abolished and replaced by other existing municipal agencies that would be responsible to elected officials.

(f) On the national level, it was recommended that the Public Housing Administration be abolished as a separate administrative program and combined with the Federal Housing Administration; the desired goal was the establishment of an agency with the ability and authority to institute and regulate a coordinate program.

Unquestionably, these suggested changes reflect dissatisfaction with many of the apparent existing deficiencies of the public housing program, for they are all aimed at corrections. Most are recommendations for drastic change, but regardless of the severity of the indictment, they are significant because they reflect actual objective analysis.

The characteristic pattern of human progress is one of trial and error; actual advance seems to occur when basic faults are discovered in some existing social, economic, or political mechanism and attempts are made to improve it by modification or substitution. Progress in the solution of adequate housing for the low-income group has been retarded by the clouds of controversy which have characterized the public housing program's evolution to date. The battle

219. Ibid.

between the extensionists and the extinctionists has not left much room for objective analysis, but with the apparent shift in sentiment noted previously, a step toward true progress will probably occur. Since the process of trial and error must result in objective discussion and the analysis of possible alternative approaches, the discussions currently taking place hold promise of much-needed progress.

The difficulty of predicting the future of low-rent housing as a public policy program is evident, but two factors indicate the general course it must take. First, a great many persons connected with urban land problems acknowledge that a stratum of low-income families requiring housing assistance is inevitable and that this aid must be furnished by some public policy program if urban renewal is to be an effective tool in municipal regeneration.

Second, this low-rent housing program should be capable of integration with other programs dealing with urban renewal problems since, "the urban renewal concept was a recognition of the tight interrelationship between zoning, planning, public housing, redevelopment and rehabilitation."[220] Mr. Bernard Loshbough, executive director of the Allegheny Conference to Improve our Neighborhoods (A.C.T.I.O.N. Housing, Inc.), has summarized the existing situation as follows:

> Sporadic housing, redevelopment and code enforcement programs on a shotgun basis will neither cure slums or blight nor prevent their growth. . . . Urban renewal demands more than piecemeal treatment. It requires community understanding and acceptance—acceptance by local leaders in business, industry, government, labor, religious and civic affairs, in trade and finance. . . . We must . . . recognize that a supply of adequate housing is essential not only to the social structure of the community, but also to its continued industrial stability and future expansion.[221]

Unquestionably, public housing has served a good purpose by focusing attention on the problem of decent housing for the low-income group and by doing something about it. In this role it can continue to be useful. The results of this study, however, indicate that the scope of any program which attempts to solve the housing problem of the low-income group must embrace the practicalities of time and finance. These conclusions seem to lend force to arguments in favor of a more general "rent subsidy" program.

---

220. James W. Rouse, "The Highways and Urban Growth," The New Highways: Challenge to the Metropolitan Region (Washington, November, 1957), p. 25.

221. Bernard Loshbough, "Urban Renewal is a New Focus for Old Functions," An Address Presented at the 1957 Annual Meeting, Pennsylvania Planning Association, November 15, 1957.

CHAPTER NINE

# The Rent Subsidy Program

The writer believes that a better solution to the problem of adequate housing for the low-income group can be approached by replacing the present expensive subsidy of a few with a smaller subsidy of the many low-income families. This change involves the shift of subsidy funds from the erection of public housing projects to a direct subsidy of a low-income family's rent bill. A rent subsidy plan is not necessarily the solution to the problem; but the plan does appear to have sufficient merit to warrant a limited trial and, if this is successful, a full-scale trial.

## Operation of the Plan

*Rental Supervision.*

Supervision of the program can be accomplished by using existing agencies handling welfare cases and those administering public housing projects or by creating a new non-political agency for this purpose. The principal function of the agency would be to operate the rent subsidy plan in the specific community. The agency should be equipped with a competent staff to investigate thoroughly each applicant for a rent subsidy and each property participating in the program.

*Selection of Tenants.*

When the eligibility of a family has been determined, the agency would grant a rent subsidy equal to the difference between the amount that the applicant is able to pay and the amount of the actual rent to be charged, providing such rental conforms to previously approved and controlled rent schedules. The applicant would be required to file certified monthly income reports subject to continuous investigation and verification. If a subsidized family is found to have income above the legal limits, such as 3-1/2 times the rent of the quarters they occupy, the rent subsidy would be stopped automatically and the family would be required to meet the rent bill out of its own income.

All tenants of all existing and any future public housing would be required to pay prevailing rentals; such rentals would be used to meet full operating costs and fixed charges, including full taxes on the assessed value of the project. Such public housing projects would be available only to those in the legal low-income bracket who have made application and have been approved for a rent subsidy.

*Selection of Properties.*

Privately-owned housing should be admitted into the plan on a voluntary basis. It would have to meet minimum housing standards to be established by the local community. Private housing in surrounding communities not having similar codes could be judged on the basis of codes existing in the nearest urban area. Rehabilitated housing and any other residential properties which could qualify on the basis of minimum standards and approved rent schedules would be eligible for tenants approved as under-legal-limit families.

The plan would include an established profit limit for the landlord of private housing participating in the plan. This limit would allow a reasonable rate of return, perhaps a 7 per cent rate of return on a property's appraised value.

## The Scope of the Proposed Program

The ramifications of this proposed program are wide in scope and, in the writer's opinion, attack the problem at its core. Briefly, the main advantages of the program are as follows:

(a) The program would take care of a very much larger share of the needy, under-legal-limit income families, whereas public housing, as it now exists, will never take care of more than a small percentage.

(b) The geographic location of available housing for the low-income group would be broadened tremendously. A few isolated projects would be replaced by available housing in many sections.

(c) The plan should help to stabilize the rental schedule of the entire community and thereby aid in stabilization of the municipal economy.

(d) The plan should serve as an impetus to the rehabilitation of substandard housing. Property owners desirous of making their properties eligible under the plan would be encouraged to make their property conform to the minimum standards.

(e) The cost of the plan should be partially offset by additional tax revenues from both the public housing projects and the rehabilitated dwelling units.

(f) In addition, the plan should help to alleviate a problem which the writer found prevalent in the survey slum areas. Slum dwellers, by and large, pay exorbitant rents for the quarters they occupy, even though they may realize that they are being exploited. The rent subsidy plan should help to correct this exploitation, first by making housing conform to an approved rental schedule and to minimum health standards and, second, by broadening the market of available decent housing for these families.

The main and obvious disadvantage of such a program is that it still requires a government subsidy. The writer recognizes this fact, but nevertheless endorses this plan for the following reason: the subsidization of housing by Government has become an established policy. Government must help if needy families are to be uprooted from their slum residence to make way for municipal regeneration in the form of slum clearance, neighborhood preservation, and urban redevelopment.

Other stated disadvantages of a rent subsidy plan may be summarized as follows:[222]

(a) A rent subsidy program would create a "dole" for housing, without contributing any tangible new housing, such as the addition of units through the building of public housing projects.

(b) A rent subsidy plan would force a great number of families to go on relief ". . . despite the fact that it is only decent housing that they cannot obtain for themselves.[223]

(c) Limiting the cost of such a program is not possible.

(d) The administrative machinery necessary to administer the program would be so huge that the ". . . program would fall of its own weight."[224]

(e) The requirement that the plan depend upon the proper enforcement of local housing and sanitation codes would militate against the low-income, owner-occupant of housing which does not conform, because he will not be able to afford the expense of necessary repairs.

---

222. The most comprehensive examination of a rent subsidy plan was undertaken in the fall of 1953 by the President's Advisory Committee on Government Housing Policies and Programs. The Committee delved into the legislative background of prior rent subsidy plans placed before Congress as well as the more fundamental considerations of program feasibility and adaptability. Included in its final report were objections to the substitution of a rent subsidy plan for the public housing program. The disadvantages listed were taken from the Committee's report. See: The President's Advisory Committee on Government Housing Policies and Programs, A Report to the President of the United States (Washington, 1953), p. 262.

223. Ibid.

224. Ibid.

(f) So much "red tape" would be involved in such a program that private enterprise would be unwilling to participate in it.

The writer believes that most of the stated disadvantages of a rent subsidy plan can be advantages. This conclusion is based on a concept of housing subsidy which envisions society's primary responsibility in a low-rent housing program as that of providing as many units of decent, sanitary housing as possible and financially practical. Further, the writer believes that private and public enterprise can join in the experimental institution of a mutually acceptable rent subsidy program having an attainable goal: the provision of a decent living environment for every American family. A rent subsidy program seems to offer the common denominator to reconcile public and private interests. Most important, it appears within the realm of experimental practicality.

The first disadvantage of the program, that it would be recognized openly as a gift, a "dole," does not seem consistent with past and still prevailing Governmental policy. The philosophy of a rent subsidy is like that of other Governmental subsidies and seems consistent with the prevailing economic and social doctrines of American free enterprise.

The institution of a rent subsidy program would result in a substantial addition of sound, decent housing to the low-income family's rental market. This increase would be achieved through the enforcement of the community's housing code; conformity would be encouraged through the opportunity to participate in the rent certificate program. True, a rent subsidy program might not encourage the addition of a substantial number of new units, but even Government subsidy of the past has failed on this count. The inability of the public housing program to provide a significant number of new units, relative to existing demand, is perhaps the program's most serious shortcoming. The cost of adding enough new units to approximate the needs of the low-income group is prohibitive.

Every housing act containing public housing authorizations has emphasized that fundamental reliance was to be placed on private enterprise—government activity being restricted to those areas where private enterprise could or would not participate. A rent certificate program provides the opportunity for Government to implement this stated principle by positive action.

The rent subsidy program holds promise of creating within the foreseeable future additional decent rental units for low-income families on a scope which even the most ardent public housing advocate cannot foresee for his program. Thus, many families now living in substandard units could look forward to occupying sanitary quarters within a relatively short time, compared to the time required for the addition of new public housing units. The addition of units under the rent subsidy program will be achieved through the rejuvenation of urban areas, not at the direct expense of all taxpaying property owners in the urban area.

The supposed disadvantage of placing low-income families "on relief" by use of a rent subsidy implies that housing aid should be concealed and that families should not be made to feel that their housing subsidy is in the form of a relief payment. Such criticism, however, seems to ignore the "stigma" which is attached inevitably to a family tenanting a public housing unit. The aura of relief is very real, and it is accentuated by the consolidation of these families within the limited confines of a project area.

If, however, the concept of relief is accepted as being more pronounced in a rent subsidy program, this so-called disadvantage could be one of the plan's prime advantages. A housing-aid program should not create an avenue of least resistance for the low-income tenant. If families are reluctant to participate in a rent subsidy program because of its relief aspects, indications would be that those families who do apply for aid have an earnest need for assistance. In addition, if the feeling of being on relief is distasteful, would this not serve as an inducement to the rental subsidy family to improve its own economic position as rapidly as possible and extinguish the necessity for aid? The writer believes that it would.

A further criticism of a rent subsidy program is that it would militate against the low-income, owner-occupant of substandard housing due to his inability to secure rehabilitation financing. The writer has emphasized the necessity of providing a means for obtaining such funds.[225] If private enterprise sincerely wishes to abolish the present system of public housing, it can furnish proof of its sincerity by the provision of loan funds, at reasonable rates of interest, for the rehabilitation of structurally sound, but substandard, houses. Available statistics indicate, however, that a relatively small percentage of slum housing is owner-occupied.[226] Nevertheless, this group, no matter how small, cannot be overlooked.

Some authorities have reacted adversely to the rent subsidy plan because it would enable a low-income, owner-occupant, by virtue of the subsidy, to build up an equity in his property which he could later dispose of for cash.[227] If this were so, the writer fails to see how such a situation could be a serious disadvantage. If the owner-occupant is industrious enough to rehabilitate his property and build up his equity, eventually he will no longer be eligible for rental aid. The result will be the rehabilitated dwelling and a rehabilitated owner-occupant. If he should decide to convert his equity into cash, is this such a disadvantage? The weight of logic seems to indicate the contrary.

---

225. Supra, p. 118.
226. Surveys in the Lower Hill Redevelopment Area in the City of Pittsburgh revealed that out of a total sample of 3580 families and individuals, 299 were owners, including 249 families and 50 individuals. See: The Pittsburgh Housing Association, Census Survey, Lower Hill Redevelopment Project (Pittsburgh, 1953), p. 10.
227. President's Advisory Committee, op. cit., p. 264.

Although the total cost of a rent subsidy program has no definite limits because of the impossibility of ascertaining the number of families to be served and the period in which the program will be operating, the program does offer the distinct advantage of being relatively easy to discontinue when the need for it decreases or no longer exists. In addition, the recommended program makes full utilization of all existing agencies concerned with the problem of relief for low-income families, including welfare agencies and the administrative staffs of local housing authorities. Therefore, if establishing such a program should prove feasible, both the problem of initiating it and effectively administering it should be reduced considerably.

The recommended subsidy program is based on the assumption that a community will enact a housing code setting forth minimum structural and sanitation standards. Many of the nation's urban communities have already enacted such comprehensive codes. The program assumes that a community will actively enforce its code and encourage the creation of adequate financing facilities as an aid to enforcement.

The need for code enforcement is evident. Investigatory activities will be required, regardless of the manner in which the Federal Government chooses to administer rental aid to low-income families. The recommended program of direct rent subsidies seeks to take advantage of this fact by offering the owners of non-conforming housing an additional incentive to comply.

Optimum results in slum eradication can be achieved by only one means—the application of a well-planned and executed housing program which has as its ultimate goal the creation and preservation of a sanitary and healthful living environment for every citizen. The community, acting through its duly-elected and appointed officials, must, therefore, pay particular heed to the preservation of all existing structures that are economically capable of salvation. With continuing emphasis placed on the extinction of blight, the physical aspects of a sanitary living environment seem assured.

To implement the attainment of this environment by low-income families, the writer recommends the initiation of a program of direct rent subsidy on a scale which will permit its proper testing and evaluation. If such analysis should demonstrate the feasibility of a rent subsidy program, a transition process should be instituted which would have as its objective the substitution of this program for the present public housing program.

Public and private enterprise must unite in the institution and support of a program capable of implementing their previous efforts. The writer offers the above program in the hope that it can serve such a purpose.

## APPENDIX I

### Public Housing Projects and Eligibility Regulations for Occupancy Housing Authority of the City of Pittsburgh As of December, 1956

Communities:

1. Addison Terrace . . . . . . . . . . . . . . . . . . . . . 802 Dwellings
2. Allegheny Dwellings . . . . . . . . . . . . . . . . . . 282 Dwellings
3. Allequippa Terrace . . . . . . . . . . . . . . . . . . .1851 Dwellings
4. Arlington Heights . . . . . . . . . . . . . . . . . . . 660 Dwellings
5. Bedford Dwellings . . . . . . . . . . . . . . . . . . . 880 Dwellings
6. Broadhead Manor . . . . . . . . . . . . . . . . . . . 448 Dwellings
7. Glen-Hazel Heights . . . . . . . . . . . . . . . . . . 999 Dwellings
8. St. Clair Village . . . . . . . . . . . . . . . . . . . .1089 Dwellings
9. (North View Heights) . . . . . . . . . . . . . . . . . 999 Dwellings
   (under construction)

Room Sizes and Occupancy:

| Room Size* | Occupancy | |
|---|---|---|
| | Not Less Than | Not More Than |
| 3 Rooms | 2 Persons | 3 Persons |
| 4 Rooms | 2 Persons | 5 Persons |
| 5 Rooms | 4 Persons | 7 Persons |
| 6 Rooms | 6 Persons | 9 Persons |
| 7 Rooms | 8 Persons | 11 Persons |

(*All dwellings include living room, bathroom and a kitchen equipped with a stove and an electric refrigerator, except Glen-Hazel Heights which has not yet been provided with refrigerators.)

Technical Requirements for Admission:

| | Initial Occupancy | Continued Occupancy |
|---|---|---|
| 1. Total Family Income Must Not Exceed: | | |
| 2 Member Family . . . . . . . . . . . . . | $3200 | $4000 |
| 3 and 4 Member Family . . . . . . . . | 3400 | 4250 |
| 5 and 6 Member Family . . . . . . . . | 3600 | 4500 |
| 7 and more Member Family . . . . . | 3800 | 4750 |

2. These limits are net income after allowing a deduction of $100.00 per minor dependent as provided in the Housing Act of 1949. A minor is a child under 21 years of age. The following payments to veterans will not be considered in computing these limits:

   a. Disability pension where disability is service connected.

   b. Payments for death to family of a deceased veteran whose death is service connected.

   c. State bonus and National Service Life Insurance refunds.

   Yearly rent charged for dwellings is approximately 20 per cent of the total family net income (including Veteran Disability Pensions and payments for death of Veteran). Rent is paid in monthly payments. Rent includes utilities.

3. Housing Need: Referrals for vacancies are determined on the basis of the relative need of the family as compared to other families.

   a. Major Factors:
      1. Living within the site of a public housing, urban redevelopment or urban renewal project.
      2. Living in a structure condemned by a public body (i.e., in violation of the Housing Code, in path of public project such as highway construction, etc.)
      3. Eviction, where it is due to no fault of the family.
      4. Substandard housing.
      5. Families having no home.
      6. Veteran or Serviceman is head of family or is living with his family.

   b. Minor Factors:
      1. Health.
      2. Number of minor children.
      3. Exceptionally low income.

   c. Veteran Priorities: In cases of a choice between families, the following priority is made in the order indicated:
      1. Disabled Veteran of World War I or II.

2. Family of deceased Veteran of World War I or II whose death was service connected.
3. Honorably discharged Veteran of World War I or II and family of man now in Military Service.
4. Non-Veteran.

Note: A Veteran or Service Man is defined as a person who is or has been in the Armed Services between April 6, 1917 and prior to November 11, 1918, September 16, 1940 and prior to July 26, 1947; and June 27, 1950 and prior to February 1, 1955.

## APPENDIX II

Housing Authority of the City of Pittsburgh
Statement of Land, Structures, and Equipment
as of
December 31, 1955

| PROJECT NUMBER | PA-1-1 | PA-1-2 | PA-1-3 | PA-1-4 | PA-1-5 | PA-1-6 | PA-1-7 | PA-1-8 | PA-1-10 |
|---|---|---|---|---|---|---|---|---|---|
| NUMBER OF DWELLING UNITS | 802 | 420 | 1,851 | 660 | 282 | 448 | 1,089 | 460 | 999 |
| ITEM | | | | | | | | | |
| Indirect development costs | $ 345,249 | $ 207,003 | $ 702,216 | $ 268,677 | $ 115,026 | $ 157,557 | $ 970,809 | $ 574,149 | $ - |
| Site acquisition | 456,940 | 313,014 | 1,308,646 | 98,997 | 81,644 | 60,690 | 562,109 | 852,204 | 62,429 |
| Excess property | - | - | - | - | - | - | - | - | - |
| Site improvement | 1,065,727 | 366,854 | 2,277,976 | 573,113 | 338,535 | 477,754 | 1,783,730 | 741,713 | 1,365,256 |
| Dwelling structures | 2,542,048 | 1,432,451 | 5,054,587 | 2,546,016 | 1,074,474 | 1,868,765 | 9,278,153 | 4,094,348 | 3,631,752 |
| Dwelling equipment—Nonexpendable | 84,264 | 44,270 | 189,006 | 96,481 | 45,699 | 49,227 | 174,180 | 75,295 | 27,898 |
| Dwelling equipment—Expendable | 18,754 | 11,072 | 47,103 | 20,666 | 9,529 | - | 46,936 | 9,258 | 11,235 |
| Nondwelling structures | 165,438 | 114,584 | 446,154 | 86,748 | 47,239 | 80,266 | 91,853 | 47,162 | 154,500 |
| Office furniture and equipment | 17,017 | 10,186 | 36,122 | 12,041 | 8,419 | 3,408 | 11,627 | 6,330 | 8,643 |
| Maintenance equipment | 581 | 256 | 4,905 | 1,856 | 259 | 1,169 | 5,286 | 3,506 | 818 |
| Community space equipment | 2,389 | 966 | 4,729 | 1,595 | 889 | 261 | 68,412 | 6,303 | 1,105 |
| Automotive equipment | 4,215 | 1,623 | 6,356 | 6,197 | - | 3,986 | 4,495 | - | 2,856 |
| Nondwelling equipment—Expendable | 5,962 | 2,736 | 13,736 | 4,052 | 2,952 | 1,177 | 2,488 | 524 | 2,977 |
| TOTAL: Land, Structures, and Equipment | $4,708,584 | $2,505,015 | $10,091,509 | $3,716,439 | $1,724,665 | $2,704,260 | $13,000,078 | $6,410,792 | $5,269,469 |

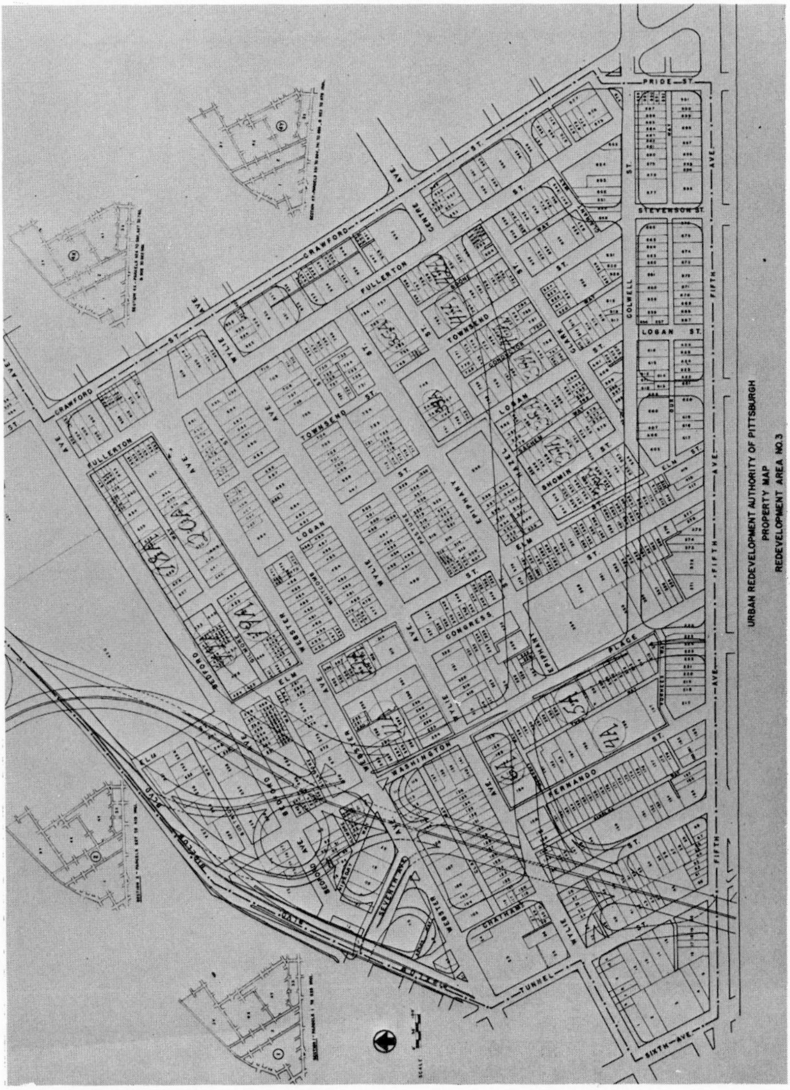
URBAN REDEVELOPMENT AUTHORITY OF PITTSBURGH
PROPERTY MAP
REDEVELOPMENT AREA NO.3
CRAWFORD ST.
FULLERTON
CENTRE AVE
WYLIE AVE
TOWNSEND ST.
LOGAN ST.
ELM ST.
WEBSTER AVE
BEDFORD AVE
EPIPHANY
CONGRESS
WASHINGTON
FERNANDO
COLWELL ST.
STEVENSON ST.
PRIDE ST.
FIFTH AVE
SIXTH AVE
TUNNEL
CHATHAM
SEVENTH AVE.
CLARK ST.
SHOWIN

FIGURE VI

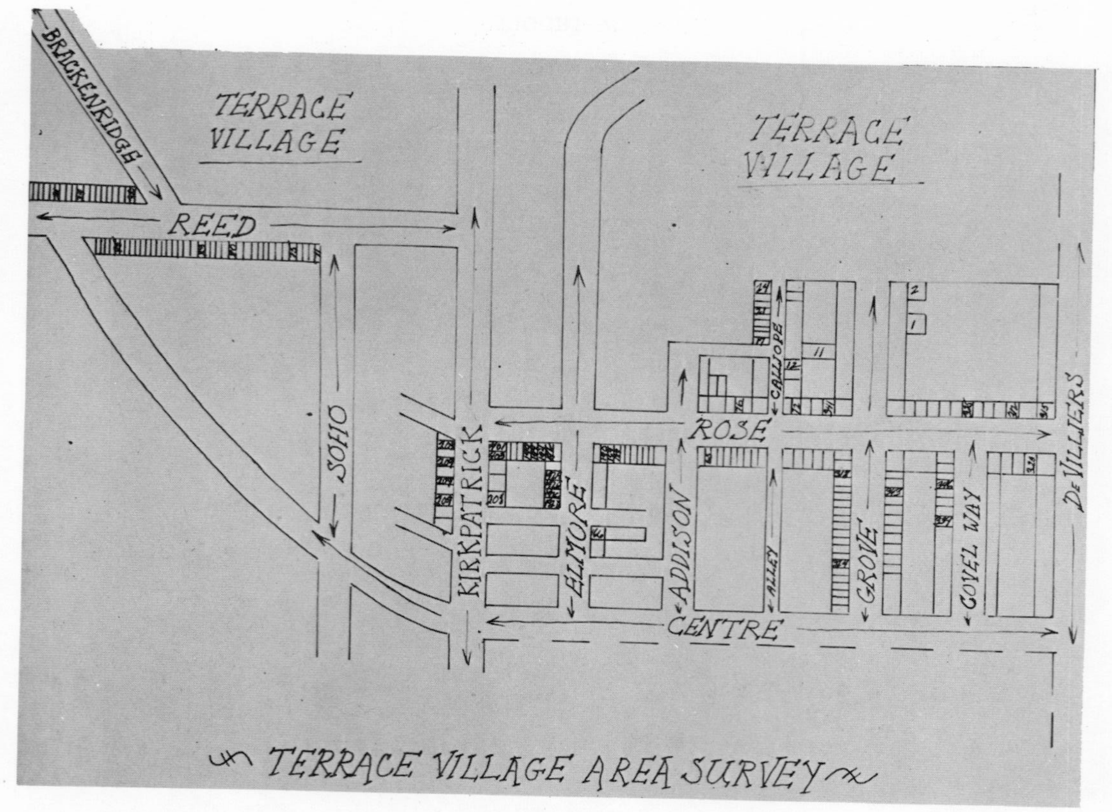
TERRACE VILLAGE
TERRACE VILLAGE
BRACKENRIDGE
REED
SOHO
KIRKPATRICK
ELMORE
ADDISON
ALLEY
CALLIOPE
ROSE
GROVE
COVEL WAY
DeVILLIERS
CENTRE
TERRACE VILLAGE AREA SURVEY

FIGURE VII

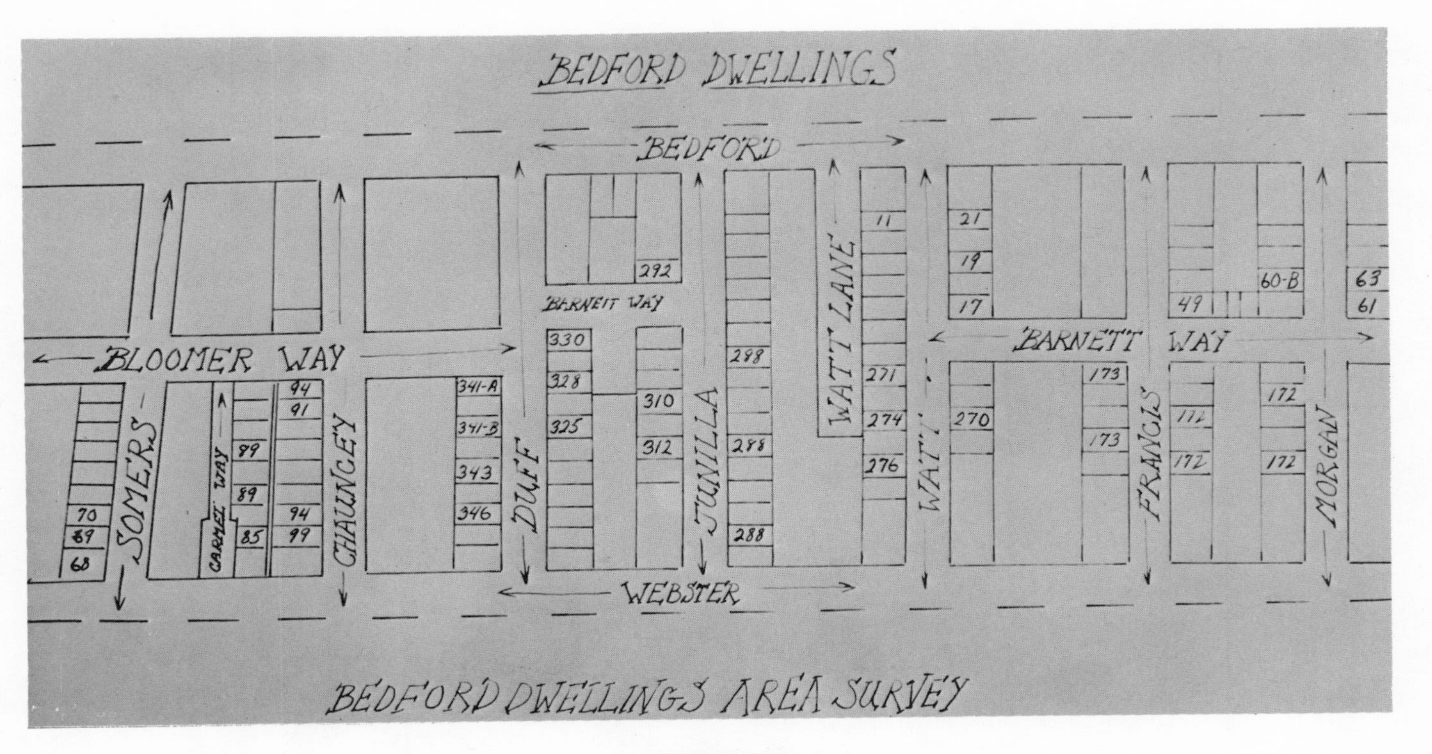
BEDFORD DWELLINGS
BEDFORD
BLOOMER WAY
BARNEIT WAY
BARNETT WAY
SOMERS
CARMEL WAY
CHAUNCEY
DUFF
JUNILLA
WATT LANE
WATT
FRANCIS
MORGAN
WEBSTER
BEDFORD DWELLINGS AREA SURVEY
70
89
68
89
89
85
94
91
94
99
341-A
341-B
343
346
292
330
328
325
310
312
298
288
288
11
271
274
276
21
19
17
270
173
173
49
60-B
172
172
172
172
172
63
61

FIGURE VIII

## BIBLIOGRAPHY

Abrams, Charles. The Future of Housing. New York: Harper and Brothers, 1946.

Baldwin, Leland D. Recent American History. New York: American Book Co., 1954.

Blank, David M. The Volume of Residential Construction, 1889-1950. New York: National Bureau of Economic Research, 1954.

Colean, Miles. American Housing: Problems and Prospects. New York: Twentieth Century Fund, 1944.

________. The Impact of Government on Real Estate Finance in the United States. New York: The National Bureau of Economic Research, 1950.

Commager, Henry Steele. Documents of American History. New York: Appleton, Century, Crofts, Inc., 1948.

DeForest, Robert W. and Veiller, Lawrence. The Tenement House Problem. 2 vols. New York: The Macmillan Co., 1903.

Eberstein, William. The Law of Public Housing. Madison: University of Wisconsin Press, 1940.

Ely, Richard T., and Wehrein, George S. Land Economics. New York: The Macmillan Co., 1940.

Federal Emergency Administration of Public Works, Housing Division. Urban Housing. Washington: Government Printing Office, 1936.

Federal Housing Administration. National Housing Act, As Amended. Washington: Government Printing Office, 1951.

Federal Reserve Bank of New York. Selected Economic Indicators. New York, 1954.

Federal Reserve System, Board of Governors. Federal Reserve Charts on Bank Credit, Money Rates and Business. September, 1956.

Fitch, Morgan L. "A Realtor Says No to Public Housing." National Real Estate and Building Journal. Vol. 55, March, 1954.

Gray, George Herbert. Housing and Citizenship. New York: Reinhold Publishing Corp., 1946.

Gross, Bertram M. The Legislative Struggle: A Study in Social Combat. New York: McGraw-Hill Book Co., Inc., 1953.

Hicks, John D. A Short History of American Democracy. New York: Houghton Mifflin Co., 1949.

Hoagland, Henry E. Real Estate Principles. New York: McGraw-Hill Book Co., Inc., 1955.

Hofstadter, Richard, Miller, William, and Aaron, Daniel. The United States: The History of a Republic. New York: Prentice-Hall, Inc., 1957.

Housing Authority of the City of Pittsburgh. The First Seven Years. Pittsburgh, 1944.

________. "Public Housing in Pittsburgh," A Report to the People. Pittsburgh, 1953.

________. Letter of Transmittal. December 29, 1954.

________. Press Release, August 8, 1949.

Housing and Home Finance Agency. A Handbook of Information on Provisions of the Housing Act of 1949. Washington: Government Printing Office, 1949.

________. First Annual Report, 1947. Washington: Government Printing Office, 1948.

________. Brief Summary of the Housing Act of 1954. Washington: Government Printing Office, 1954.

________. Detailed Summary of the Housing Act of 1956. Washington: Government Printing Office, 1956.

________. Provisions of Housing Codes in Various American Cities. Urban Renewal Bulletin No. 3. Washington: Government Printing Office, 1956.

Housing Laws of Pennsylvania, 1937.

Hovde, Bryn. "Editorial." Housing News. Vol. 1. Pittsburgh: Pittsburgh Housing Association, October, 1953.

Hunter, Robert. Tenement Conditions in Chicago. Chicago: City Homes Association, 1901.

Ickes, Harold L. Back to Work. New York: The Macmillan Co., 1935.

________. The Secret Diary of Harold L. Ickes: The First Thousand Days, 1933-1936. New York: Simon and Schuster, 1953.

Keynes, John M. The General Theory of Employment, Interests and Money. New York: Harcourt, Brace and Co., 1935.

Link, Arthur S. American Epoch. New York: Alfred A. Knopf, 1955.

McGeary, M. Nelson. The Pittsburgh Housing Authority. State College: The Pennsylvania State College, 1943.

McNaughton, Frank and Hehmeyer, Walter. Harry Truman, President. New New York: Whittlesey House. McGraw-Hill Book Co., Inc., 1948.

Millspaugh, Martin. What is Urban Renewal? Washington, D.C.: New Face for American Committee of the National Association of Home Builders, 1956.

Morgan, Theodore. Income and Employment. New York: Prentice-Hall, Inc., 1954.

Murphy, John J., Wood, Edith Elmer, and Ackerman, Frederick L. The Housing Famine: How to End It. New York: E. P. Dutton and Co., 1920.

National Association of Real Estate Boards. Blueprint for Neighborhood Conservation. Henry J. Kaiser Co., 1956.

National Housing Agency. Second Annual Report, 1943. Washington: Government Printing Office, 1944.

________. Third Annual Report, 1944. Washington: Government Printing Office, 1945.

________. Fourth Annual Report, 1945. Washington: Government Printing Office, 1946.

________. Fifth Annual Report, 1946. Washington: Government Printing Office, 1947.

________. Housing for War and the Job Ahead. Washington: Government Printing Office, 1944.

________. Housing Needs. National Housing Bulletin No. 1. Washington: Government Printing Office, 1944.

Ogg, Frederic A., and Ray P. Orman. Essentials of American Government. New York: Appleton, Century, Crofts, Inc., 1950.

Perkins, Francis. The Roosevelt I Knew. New York: Viking Press, 1946.

Pittsburgh, City of. Annual Report of the City Comptroller for the Fiscal Period Ended December 31, 1955. Pittsburgh, 1956.

Pittsburgh City Council. Ordinance 338. August 26, 1937.

Pittsburgh Housing Association. Housing in Pittsburgh, 1930. Pittsburgh, 1931.

________. Housing in Pittsburgh, 1931-1933. Pittsburgh, 1933.

________. Housing in Pittsburgh, 1934-1937. Pittsburgh, 1937.

________. Housing in Pittsburgh, 1938. Pittsburgh, 1939.

________. Housing in Pittsburgh, 1939. Pittsburgh, 1940.

________. Housing in Pittsburgh, 1941-1942. Pittsburgh, 1943.

________. Housing in Pittsburgh, 1942-1943. Pittsburgh, 1944.

________. Housing in Pittsburgh, 1945-1946. Pittsburgh, 1947.

________. Housing in Pittsburgh, 1947-1951. Pittsburgh, 1952.

________. Census Survey Lower Hill Redevelopment Project, Redevelopment Area No. 3. Pittsburgh, 1953.

Pittsburgh Planning Commission, Department of City Planning. Groundwork and Inventory for the Master Plan. Pittsburgh, 1945.

The Poor in Great Cities. New York: Charles Scribner's Sons, 1895.

Post, Langdon W. The Challenge of Housing. New York: Farrar and Rinehart, Inc., 1938.

The President's Advisory Committee on Government Housing Policies and Programs. A Report to the President of the United States. Washington: Government Printing Office, 1953.

Public Housing Administration. First Annual Report, 1947. Washington: Government Printing Office, 1947.

________. Third Annual Report, 1949. Washington: Government Printing Office, 1949.

________. Fourth Annual Report, 1950. Washington: Government Printing Office, 1950.

________. Fifth Annual Report, 1951. Washington: Government Printing Office, 1951.

________. Sixth Annual Report, 1952. Washington: Government Printing Office, 1952.

________. Seventh Annual Report, 1953. Washington: Government Printing Office, 1953.

________. Eighth Annual Report, 1954. Washington: Government Printing Office, 1954.

________. Ninth Annual Report, 1955. Washington: Government Printing Office, 1955.

Ratcliff, Richard U. Urban Land Economics. New York: McGraw-Hill Book Co., Inc., 1949.

Riis, Jacob A. How the Other Half Lives. New York: Charles Scribner's Sons, 1890.

________. The Battle With the Slum. New York: The Macmillan Co., 1902.

Schlesinger, Arthur Meier. The New Deal in Action, 1933-1939. New York: The Macmillan Co., 1940.

Shattuck, Charles B. Address Before Greater Pittsburgh Board of Realtors. February, 1953.

Slusser, Charles E. "The Commissioner's Case for Public Housing." National Real Estate and Building Journal. Vol. 55. March, 1954.

Stapp, Peyton. Urban Housing, A Survey of Real Property Inventories Conducted as Work Projects, 1934-1936. Washington: Government Printing Office, 1938.

Straus, Michael W. and Wegg, Talbot. Housing Comes of Age. New York: Oxford University Press, 1938.

Strauss, Nathan. The Seven Myths of Housing. New York: Alfred A. Knopf, 1944.

________. Two-Thirds of a Nation, A Housing Program. New York: Alfred A. Knopf, 1952.

Truman, Harry S. Memoirs. 2 Vols. New York: Doubleday and Co., Inc., 1955.

University of Pittsburgh, Bureau of Business Research, Real Property Inventory of Allegheny County, Pittsburgh, 1937.

U.S. Bureau of the Census. Seventeenth Census of the United States: 1940. Population, Vol. II.

________. Eighteenth Census of the United States: 1950. Population, Vol. V. Block Statistics. Pt. 145.

________. Eighteenth Census of the United States: 1950. Housing, Vol. . Census Tract Statistics. Chap. 43.

U.S. Department of Commerce. Metropolitan Basic Data Sheets. Washington: Government Printing Office, 1947.

U.S. Department of Health, Education and Welfare. Public Health Service. Housing Rehabilitation and Enforcement of Housing Laws. Washington: Government Printing Office, 1955.

U.S. Congressional Record. Vol. LXXX.

________. Vol. LXXXI.

________. Vol. LXXXXI.

________. Vol. LXXXXII.

________. Vol. LXXXXIV.

________. Vol. LXXXXV.

________. Vol. LXXXXIX.

________. Vol. C.

________. Vol. CI.

________. Vol. CII.

U.S. House of Representatives. Committee on Banking and Currency. Hearings on H. R. 5033, S. 1685, 75th Cong., 2d Sess., 1937.

________. Hearings on S. 591. 76th Cong., 1st Sess., 1939.

________. Hearings on S. 866. 80th Cong., 2d Sess., 1948.

________. Federal Housing Programs: Chronology and Description. 81st Cong., 2d Sess., 1950.

________. Hearings on H. R. 4009. 81st Cong., 1st Sess., 1949.

U.S. House of Representatives. Your Congress and American Housing: The Actions of Congress on Housing from 1892-1951. 82d Cong., 2d Sess., 1952.

U.S. House of Representatives. Committee on Banking and Currency. Hearings on H. R. 5827—Housing Amendments of 1955. 84th Cong., 1st Sess., 1955.

________. Hearings on H.R.10157—Housing Act of 1956. 84th Cong., 2d Sess., 1956.

U.S. Senate. Committee on Education and Labor. Hearings on S. 1685. 75th Cong., 1st Sess., 1937.

U.S. Senate. Committee on Banking and Currency. Hearings Before A Subcommittee on the Housing Act of 1955. 84th Cong., 1st Sess., 1955.

U.S. Senate. Committee on Banking and Currency. Hearings Before A Subcommittee on the Housing Act of 1956. 84th Cong., 2d Sess., 1956.

U.S. Housing Authority. What the Housing Act Can Do For Your City. Washington: Government Printing Office, 1938.

Veiller, Lawrence. Housing Reform. New York: Charities Publication Committee, 1910.

Walker, Mabel L. Urban Blight and Slums. Cambridge: Harvard University Press, 1938.

Watson, J. P. The City Real Estate Tax in Pittsburgh. Pittsburgh: Bureau of Business Research, University of Pittsburgh, 1934.

Weimer, Arthur and Hoyt, Homer. Real Estate Principles. New York: Ronald Book Co., 1954.

Wenzlick, Roy. "As I See." The Real Estate Analyst. St. Louis, July 22, 1949.

Wish, Harvey. Contemporary America. New York: Harper and Brothers, Publishers, 1955.

Wood, Edith Elmer. Housing of the Unskilled Wage Earner. New York: The Macmillan Co., 1919.